PRAISE

A CHANGE OF A

"This short book is a very healthy mixture of candid self-disclosure and rigorous thought. It combines good storytelling with careful handling of the Bible. It is always honest and never glib. In the rising tide of literature on same-sex attraction and homosexuality, this book stands out as one of the most constructive."

—D. A. Carson, founder and president of the Gospel Coalition

"*A Change of Affection* is one of the most powerful, awe-inspiring stories I have ever read. It will bring you to tears, strengthen your confidence in God's power to change lives, and create in you a greater hunger to make Jesus the Lord of your life. The book is just flat-out hard to put down! It is not only interesting and inspirational, but Becket Cook also teaches us a lot about the nature and importance of discipleship unto the Lord Jesus. Put simply, it is a biblically and transformationally rich account of Cook's incredible journey. I highly recommend it."

—J. P. Moreland, distinguished professor of philosophy at Talbot School of Theology and author of *Finding Quiet: My Story of Overcoming Anxiety and the Practices That Brought Peace*

"Are Christians enemy number one of the gay community? Is disagreement an expression of hatred, as my culture wants to claim? This attractive book tells a very different story, and a far more realistic one. It starts with a bang: Becket meeting a so-called Bible Guy, whose answers to his skeptical questions regarding Christianity are surprisingly thoughtful, and a sermon so enlightening that a newcomer like Becket didn't want it to end (imagine). And as valuable as anything is Part 2: Reflections, where Cook demonstrates a great heart and mind."

—Dick Lucas, rector emeritus, St. Helen's Church, Bishopsgate, London

"*A Change of Affection* is a riveting book. I couldn't put it down. With conviction, clarity, and compassion, Becket shares his remarkable story in a manner that will inspire believers and challenge seekers. I truly hope this book is widely read and discussed, because it offers a powerful story of redemption and hope in our lonely and hurting world."

—Sean McDowell, PhD, professor at Biola University, popular speaker, and author of *So the Next Generation Will Know*

"Becket Cook has written an honest, wise, moving, and compelling account of being a gay man who eventually discovers his fullest life and deepest love in Jesus Christ. I found it inspiring!"

—Sam Allberry, speaker for Ravi Zacharias International Ministries and author of *Is God Anti-Gay?*

"Written from the same divine love that overwhelmed and captured him, Becket Cook's *A Change of Affection* is compelling wisdom for skeptics and believers alike. It is full of what James 3:17 calls the 'wisdom from above [that] is first pure, then peaceable, gentle, reasonable, full of mercy and good fruits, unwavering, without hypocrisy.' Such treasures await the reader on every page. Wherever the issue of homosexuality touches your life, there will be profit from Cook's account of meeting and probing the depths of love of the Living God for you."

—Mark R. Saucy, professor and co-chair at Talbot School of Theology

"*A Change of Affection* is a tour de force. Becket Cook's story will pull on your heartstrings and engage your theological mind. More than that, you'll be inspired to share Jesus with your LGBTQ loved ones. This is a must read!"

—Caleb Kaltenbach, founder of the Messy Grace Group and author of *Messy Grace* and *God of Tomorrow*

"In Hollywood, fortune favors the bold. So when I saw Becket for the first time on his knees, I thought, *What is this smart, handsome, and successful guy doing in church?* Becket's transformation and sacrificial humility to boldly stand for Jesus Christ for a time such as this is powerful and timely! *A Change of Affection* is a change in direction for the next several generations and beyond."

    —Stephen Baldwin, actor, author, and evangelist

"Sexuality is one of the most important, yet misunderstood topics in our society today. Thankfully, in a sound-bite culture filled with vitriolic exchanges, Becket Cook has offered a perspective that is deeply personal, biblically grounded, and winsomely practical. As one of Becket's pastors in Los Angeles, I can say that his life truly is a display of God's grace and that the words in this book reflect a living and embodied faith in Christ. I hope many read *A Change of Affection*, and I trust that the church will be built up as a result."

    —Jeremy Treat, PhD, pastor at Reality LA, adjunct professor of theology at Biola University, and author of *Seek First* and *The Crucified King*

A CHANGE OF AFFECTION

A
CHANGE OF
AFFECTION

A Gay Man's Incredible
Story of Redemption

BECKET COOK

NELSON
BOOKS

An Imprint of Thomas Nelson

Published in Nashville, Tennessee, by Nelson Books, an imprint of Thomas Nelson. Nelson Books and Thomas Nelson are registered trademarks of HarperCollins Christian Publishing, Inc.

Published in association with Don Gates—The Gates Group, www.the-gates-group.com.

Thomas Nelson titles may be purchased in bulk for educational, business, fund-raising, or sales promotional use. For information, please e-mail SpecialMarkets@ThomasNelson.com.

AUTHOR'S NOTE: This is a work of nonfiction. The events and experiences described are all true and have been faithfully rendered as I have remembered them to the best of my ability. I have also changed the names, identities, and circumstances of some of the people depicted in order to protect their privacy.

Library of Congress Cataloging-in-Publication Data

Names: Cook, Becket, 1967- author.
Title: A change of affection : a gay man's incredible story of redemption / by Becket Cook.
Description: Nashville : Thomas Nelson, 2019.
Identifiers: LCCN 2018056013 (print) | LCCN 2019007899 (ebook) | ISBN 9781400212347 (e-book) | ISBN 9781400212309 (pbk.)
Subjects: LCSH: Cook, Becket, 1967- | Christian converts--California--Biography. | Homosexuality--Religious aspects--Christianity.
Classification: LCC BV4935.C634 (ebook) | LCC BV4935.C634 A3 2019 (print) | DDC 261.8/357662092 [B] --dc23
LC record available at https://lccn.loc.gov/2018056013

Printed in the United States of America

22 LSC 11

To my family,
for praying for me unceasingly for all those years.

CONTENTS

CONTENTS

FOREWORD

I literally screamed the first time I heard Becket speak. I think I've only done that twice in my life. I normally like to hide in crowds silently, but he said something that caused me to shout before I could restrain myself.

In 2015, my wife and I were crammed into a room in San Francisco, where people flooded to hear Becket share his life story and answer questions. Many were intrigued by the stories about his past, but that's not what shocked me. It was his demeanor. It was the way he demonstrated an obsession with Jesus. He carried himself like a man who had just won the lottery; like someone who was unfazed by the parking ticket he received, because he discovered his newfound fortune and was amazed at the treasure he had been given. Everything else seemed trivial to him, even his sexuality.

It reminded me of the scene in the Bible when Jesus entered the home of Zacchaeus (Luke 19). Zacchaeus was so overjoyed that he tells Jesus he will give half of all his money to the poor and then repay anyone he has stolen from—quadruple the amount! His riches meant nothing to him if he could have Jesus. And Christ responded, "Today salvation has come to this house" (v. 9). Zacchaeus suddenly had little regard for the money he had treasured his entire life, because he received something infinitely greater.

Today, that kind of response would stand out as exceptionally zealous in much of the American church community. Although, in reality, Zacchaeus's response was perfectly appropriate. It was the response of a true believer, and the kind of response Jesus expects.

In Matthew 13:44, Jesus said, "The kingdom of heaven is like treasure hidden in a field, which a man found and covered up. Then in his joy he goes and sells all that he has and buys that field." God expects us to be obsessed with Him. To see Him as so valuable that we would eagerly give up anything and everything to be part of His Kingdom. It's refreshing to see that kind of enthusiasm in Becket, especially in America where God is often viewed as an obligation, or even a nuisance.

Much of what Becket writes in this book will seem like utter nonsense, unless you understand what he means when he uses the word God. The picture he has in his mind when he uses that word is probably different from what you are imagining right now. It's only when you get a glimpse of Becket's view of God that you can understand how he reaches his conclusions about life and sexuality.

Erase whatever picture of God you have in your mind, and consider this description of Him from the pages of the Bible:

> For you have not come to what may be touched, a blazing fire and darkness and gloom and a tempest and the sound of a trumpet and a voice whose words made the hearers beg that no further messages be spoken to them. For they could not endure the order that was given, "If even a beast touches the mountain, it shall be stoned." Indeed, so terrifying was the sight that Moses said, "I tremble with fear." But you have come to Mount Zion and to the city of the living God, the heavenly Jerusalem, and to innumerable angels in festal gathering, and to the assembly of the firstborn who are enrolled in heaven, and to God, the judge of all, and to the spirits of the righteous made perfect, and to Jesus, the mediator of a new covenant, and to the sprinkled blood that speaks a better word than the blood of Abel. (Heb. 12:18–24)

Imagine standing in an open field as a massive hurricane comes raging toward you. Your riches matter very little at that point. No matter how much power or intellect you may have, you are helpless. God equates Himself to a "tempest." Hebrews explains that we are not dealing with a normal person. He is untouchable. He is a "blazing fire and darkness" all at once. Present day Bible teachers don't use words like "gloom and a tempest" to describe Him. Many Christians casually speak of how they want to hear His voice, not taking into account that those who had heard Him "[begged] that no further messages be spoken." We have forgotten that Moses was terrified and "[trembled] with fear." We are speaking of the "living judge of all," who dwells in heaven with "innumerable angels" celebrating Him.

Now imagine standing in the presence of a Being with all those attributes and more. Imagine that holy, awesome God declaring you to be His child and loving you as such. Your position as a beloved child of God would become the only identity you care to have.

Becket's testimony that day was so powerful to me because he spoke as though he genuinely believed he was *that loved* by a person *that great*. Basking in the wonder of that incredible truth, all the pleasures of earth grew dim.

There's another story in scripture that stands in stark contrast to Zacchaeus and the parable of the hidden treasure. In Luke 18, Jesus encounters a rich young ruler. Jesus asked him to sell all that he had in order to follow Him, but instead the man walked away sadly. Unlike Zacchaeus or the man who found the treasure in the field, this young man felt like there was a decision to be made. The fact that he even had to think about it showed that he didn't understand the worth of Christ.

This is the prevailing attitude toward God today. Most are not sure if He is worth the sacrifice that He requires. Some try to ignore or diminish the demands of Jesus:

Whoever loves father or mother more than me is not worthy of me, and whoever loves son or daughter more than me is not worthy of me. And whoever does not take his cross and follow me is not worthy of me. Whoever finds his life will lose it, and whoever loses his life for my sake will find it. (Matt. 10:37–39)

The world is populated by men and women, like the rich young ruler, who cannot see the true value of God. They refuse to "lose their life" because they consider themselves valuable and God ancillary. Becket's story is the rare example of a person who gladly let go of everything he had to find a greater life.

Francis Chan
New York Times bestselling
author of *Crazy Love*

PART ONE

TO THE LIGHTHOUSE

ONE

BEING THERE

September 12, 2009, was a typical Saturday in Los Angeles for me: wake up late, drive from West Hollywood to Venice Beach to meet my best friend, Ryan, for brunch at our favorite understated and overpriced farm-to-table restaurant, and then drive across town to Silver Lake to continue our lazy day at Intelligentsia, a local artisanal coffee bar. On our way to the Eastside, we would usually shop at various clothing stores on Abbot Kinney Boulevard or trek over to Beverly Hills and hit Barneys or drop in at Fred Segal and Maxfield in West Hollywood. The perennially perfect LA weather, seventy-five and sunny, was just the right climate for these breezy, carefree days. As afternoon moved into evening, we would likely find our way to another favorite upscale restaurant for a yummy dinner.

Ryan was a successful artist, and I was a successful production designer. We had ample disposable income, which we were happy to dispose of. We never lacked ways to fill the day, and almost always had some art show or house party to attend after dinner. These Saturdays had been our sacred weekly ritual for almost a decade. On this particular Saturday, however, there was something different in the air. Something that would set off a chain of events and forever change my life.

After brunch we stood in the long line at Intelligentsia. I ordered my preferred cappuccino, and Ryan picked up his favorite floral-infused tea. We somehow scored a great table out on the patio despite the hordes of people there that day. While sipping our drinks and taking in the crowd around us, we noticed something odd, especially for that part of Los Angeles. A stylish man who may have been in his early thirties walked by our table with a to-go coffee in one hand and a large hardcover book in the other, with the title *Romans Commentary* on the spine. Though neither Ryan nor I had been involved with church in our adult lives, we knew enough to guess that this book was Bible related. But we were in Silver Lake, one of the most liberal, progressive enclaves in all of Los Angeles county.

Ryan and I gave each other a puzzled look. Who was this handsome guy, and why was he carrying this religious book? Our fascination doubled when he stopped near a handful of hipster twentysomethings, each with a Bible either in hand or on the table in front of them. What? Carrying Bibles in public in Los Angeles? I had never seen this in all my fifteen years living here. Not once.

We watched as the guy exchanged hugs and pleasantries with the group of Bible people for a few minutes before leaving. Ryan and I were baffled. Was it the coffee they drank? Was some sort of religious cult taking over Silver Lake? Were they planning a trip to Jonestown, Guyana? After a bit of speculative discussion, we resumed our normal chitchat, occasionally glancing over at the group for any new developments. Then we noticed everyone at the table bowing their heads and beginning to pray. In truth, we were half-disgusted and half-intrigued. On the religion scale, we were both somewhere between agnostic and atheist. God was never mentioned in our circles, and if religion ever came up in conversation, it was invariably with contempt and suspicion. After several minutes the prayer ended, and, except for one guy, everyone got up, said goodbye, and headed off.

Ryan, always game for a controversial conversation, urged me to ask the remaining guy what he and his companions had been up to. I refused, but he goaded me, probably because he wanted to liven up our stale colloquy. After a resistant sigh, I finally turned to the Bible Guy, "Excuse me. Hi. Um . . . are you a Christian or . . ."

"Yes." His reply was quick and confident.

After an awkward pause, Ryan and I turned our chairs to join his table. He smiled, apparently fine with our intrusion. I then kick-started our dialogue; even though Ryan loved contentious discussions, he tended to hang back while I did the heavy lifting in these kinds of social situations. I explained to

Bible Guy, Colin, that I had been raised Catholic but was a bit fuzzy on the details of Christianity and the Bible. Then I just came out and asked him, "What do you actually believe?"

Turns out he was an evangelical Christian, part of a church in Hollywood called Reality LA. He was very open to explaining his faith to us, so I peppered him with questions:

- "How can you be certain God exists?"
- "How can the Bible be true?"
- "What about human suffering?"
- "What about people who reject or never even hear the gospel?"

His answers were surprisingly thoughtful. So I finally conjured the boldness to address the elephant on the patio, the biggest hang-up in my mind, the $64,000 question: "What about homosexuality? What is your church's stance on it? Is it a sin or not?"

His answer didn't shock me. He didn't beat around the bush, and very matter-of-factly stated that both he and his church agreed homosexuality is indeed a sin. Moreover, he went on to admit that he struggled with same-sex attraction too, but his convictions on this issue were settled: following Jesus was worth denying that aspect of himself.

In the past, I had typically responded to this explanation by telling the person how utterly delusional he was, how he probably needed therapy, or how he obviously had been brainwashed as a child growing up in a Christian family. But for some reason, this time it was different. I didn't feel threatened or angry or alienated. I was just surprised, and slightly confused. I also felt a strange respect for him for believing in something and having the courage to stand by it, especially something as unpopular as that. His honesty and boldness were refreshing. In my personal, postmodern world, in which all truth was subjective, I was struck by the suggestion that there could be some kind of objective truth, whether I liked it or not. I didn't have a response, which for me was rare.

Then he needed to go. But before he left, he asked Ryan and me if we'd be interested in coming to his church the following weekend. Once again, I was surprised at his gentle confidence. I accepted his invitation on the spot, probably out of politeness, because internally, I wasn't so sure. As for Ryan, it was clear from his body language that he wasn't really interested in entertaining the idea. I was on my own in this. Colin and I exchanged phone numbers and parted ways.

SHOULD I STAY OR SHOULD I GO?

In the days that followed, I had time to contemplate the implications of going to Colin's church. It didn't make any sense for me to go. First, I didn't even believe in God. Second, there is that little homosexuality glitch. As a gay man, God had never been an option for me considering he didn't approve of that sort of thing. End of story.

I also felt like I would be betraying my people. We all thought that Christians were the enemy. How could I even consider going into the den of these foes? They think being gay is wrong. They believe who I am is a sin. I've felt alienated and marginalized by them my whole life. I couldn't join that club.

But I couldn't shake the thought of going either. Something was pushing me to go. Maybe I wasn't right about everything as I thought I was. What the heck did I know anyway? Maybe there was more to life than meets the eye. What if God did exist? I guess there was that slim chance. And if he did, what implications would that have for my life? For my afterlife, if there was such a thing?

No, this is silly! I corrected myself. *Of course the Bible story is a myth, like all ancient myths and world religions. I'm no fool.* I knew and affirmed Karl Marx's shrewd explanation of religion: "Religion is the sigh of the oppressed creature, the heart of a heartless world, and the soul of soulless conditions. It is the opium of the people."[1] And even if I were drawn by some of Christianity's claims, I couldn't get past their insistence on being the *only* way. How could 1.6 billion Muslims, 500 million Buddhists, and 1.1 billion Hindus all be wrong? And people were only drawn to their religions because they happened to be born in a part of the world where that particular myth was perpetuated. Then there is the coldhearted claim about those who have never heard of the Gospels being condemned to eternal damnation. I guess they're just really unlucky?

What about science? Don't Charles Darwin's theory of evolution and Georges Lemaître's big bang theory finally and utterly render God and the Bible obsolete? Wasn't Richard Dawkins right when he said, "Faith is the great cop-out, the great excuse to evade the need to think and evaluate evidence. Faith is the belief in spite of, even perhaps because of, the lack of evidence."[2] Isn't faith in God the same as believing in Santa Claus or the Tooth Fairy? Oh, and let's not forget the really big problem: human suffering. How could a supposedly good God allow little children to get cancer and die?

Even as I wrestled with the arguments I always had against Christianity, Colin's invitation persisted in my mind. I had every reason to forget the invitation, or just text him, "Thanks, but no thanks." And if he texted me I could just ignore it, since I didn't even know the guy. We had a moderately interesting conversation is all. I told myself I was stressing out for no reason, and decided I was definitely not going and wasn't going to text him either. I didn't owe him anything.

But I still couldn't shake it. I thought, *What's the harm in at least checking this church out?* I decided to embrace it as something of an anthropological study. A chance to confirm all my suspicions about the ridiculousness of Christianity. As long as small paper cups of Kool-Aid weren't being passed around, I would be okay, right?

I, of course, didn't want any of my progressive, liberal,

sophisticated friends knowing I was considering such an act of blasphemy. In my circle of friends, Christianity was not only considered a joke, it was considered downright dangerous, especially with that whole "homosexuality is a sin" thing.

Homosexuality had finally won a place of broad acceptance in the American culture. Television shows and movies featured gay characters who were the heroes, not the villains. In the 1990s, the sitcom *Ellen*, starring Ellen DeGeneres, made television history when her character came out as a lesbian. Then came a series of hugely influential television shows and films in the late 1990s and early 2000s: *Will & Grace*, *Queer Eye for the Straight Guy*, *Brokeback Mountain*, and *Milk*, to name a few. I remember when the reality television series *Queer Eye* came out in 2003. It was something of a tipping point in our culture. Not only were gays tuning in, but straight men and women were tuning in as well! What? Straight guys were obsessed with a show about five gay guys making over style-challenged dudes? Something was up. You could just feel it in the air. The show was a game changer. And, of course, the exquisitely directed *Brokeback Mountain* moved gay acceptance up several more notches. So what was I supposed to do? I didn't sit through eight shrill seasons of *Will & Grace* for nothing!

The political terrain was changing as well, and at breakneck speed. The so-called sodomy laws were being struck down all across the nation, same-sex civil unions were now legal in several states, and gay marriage was slowly becoming a reality. So why would I want to step back in time into this anachronistic evangelical church? Had I lost my mind? Christianity was for ignorant folks in flyover states, not for coastal sophisticates, right? I would be going against who I was and everything I believed in. No thanks!

Then I got a text on Thursday from Colin asking if I was still interested in coming to church on Sunday. I bristled initially, but later realized that I was somehow still considering it. I told him I was planning to be there, even though I hadn't actually made up my mind. I had a few more days to mull it over, so I decided there wasn't any need to make a rash decision. I would wait until the day of to see how I felt.

HERE GOES

Sunday morning finally rolled around, and I woke up, showered, dressed, left my apartment, got in my car, and drove to Colin's church. I knew it was weird. I had no reason for doing it, nor had any idea what I was doing or what to expect. As I neared the church, I still couldn't believe I was doing it. I thought of turning around and going back home, but I was almost there, so decided I might as well just go in and check it out.

The service was held at a Los Angeles public high school. After I parked my car in a nearby multilevel parking garage, I walked up a flight of stairs and across a courtyard. As I neared the entrance, a woman greeted me, "Hello, we love you."

Uh-oh, maybe this is another Hollywood cult. Coincidentally, the building was just a few blocks away from the Church of Scientology Celebrity Centre.

After thanking the Loving Lady, I walked into the auditorium. The service was just beginning, and I immediately cringed when I heard Christian music being played by the worship band. *Ugh. I forgot about Christian music!* Christian worship music was something I had seen satirized on television, and something my friends and I regarded as just plain cheesy. An usher guided me to a seat near the front, and I sat down amid hundreds of believers. I was a stranger in a strange land. I might as well have been on Mars, because these Martians were earnestly singing in unison; some even had their eyes closed and hands raised in the air. *Wow. This is serious.*

But after a few songs, I didn't mind the music so much. In fact, I thought it was quite good and even tasteful. I then looked around at the brand-new, simply designed auditorium. The unadorned space, with its plain white cinder block walls, seemed very modest and uncomplicated to me. The bells and whistles I was accustomed to as a child growing up in the heavily ornamented Catholic Church were refreshingly absent.

After several more songs and a few announcements, the pastor came onstage. *That's the guy with the* Romans Commentary *book from the coffee place!* He headed to the podium, set down his Bible, and began to speak. After greeting the congregation, he prayed and read a passage from the book of Romans, chapter 7. He then began to preach.

What I heard in that sermon would completely transform my understanding of who I am, where I came from, where I'm headed, my purpose in the world, and ultimately, who God is.

TWO

DEUS EX MACHINA:
CONVERSION

It was as though a light of confidence flooded into my heart and all the darkness of doubt was dispelled.

—Augustine, Confessions

The Lord is my strength and my song,
and he has become my salvation;
this is my God, and I will praise him,
my father's God, and I will exalt him.

—Exodus 15:2

THE MOMENT OF TRUTH

On September 20, 2009—that peculiar day I found myself in an evangelical church for the first time—I sat in the auditorium, listening intently as the pastor began his sermon from the apostle Paul's letter to the Romans. I, along with the rest of the congregation, was captivated.

As he preached, every sentence that came out of his mouth resonated as truthful to me. It was strange, and I had no idea why. My thoughts kept exclaiming, *Yes, that's true . . . Yes, that's true . . . Yes, that's true!* My mind and heart were agreeing with every word he was saying, and continued to do so for the entire hour-long sermon. At one point, I remember thinking, *This is the gospel?* What he was saying was turning everything I thought I knew about religion on its head. I was stunned by the utter simplicity of it.

He opened the sermon by saying, "Most people think Christianity, or the Christian life, means being a good person and not sinning." *Yep. That's what I always thought.* As he continued, I began to realize that I had never really understood the true gospel. For the first time, I learned that a loving Creator designed us to exist in relationship with him, with each other, and with the rest of creation. Our Creator is a holy, good, and loving God. But we, humanity, turned away from him because of pride. We sought to establish our own autonomy, our own independence, and attempted to become our own god rather than trust in and depend on him. And when this happened, the very fabric of our being went awry. This is the origin of our downfall. Having rejected the very Source of our being, our hearts became twisted, self-centered, disoriented, and corrupted. All of us are born into this. We spend much of our lives pursuing our own self-interests at the expense of so many around us. Instead of living to serve others and helping them flourish, we seek our own agendas to others' destruction, as well as our own. We violate the very creatures God loves so deeply. And in the process, we all remain in enmity with our holy and good Creator.

I had seriously misunderstood the Christian religion to be all about man trying to morally perform, in his strength, to be approved by and made acceptable to God. So, he spends his life just trying to be a good person, thinking maybe if he lives a good enough life he will one day be accepted by God. But now it became clear to me that *no one* could ever perform well enough to measure up.

The overwhelming wonder of God's infinite love is this: While I was broken and a failure, God came to rescue me. He came to love me, to redeem me, and to heal me from sin. Where I failed, Christ succeeded on my behalf. Where I distrusted, Christ was faithful. Where I proudly resisted, he humbly surrendered. Through his obedience, he bridged the chasm between my darkness and his light. On the cross, God's Son took my place and became a sacrifice for all my failures. In his resurrection, he triumphed over all my destruction. And he now stands as my victorious Redeemer, offering me—and all who will simply receive him—his forgiveness and vindication. Christ clothes my shame and brokenness with his righteous and holy life.

I heard the Christian message loud and clear that day: I,

in and of myself, had nothing to give or do . . . I had only to receive. This *is* the good news.

Grasping this for the first time had me feeling that it was almost too good to be true. *No way! This is the gospel?* My heart was racing. I would never have believed that I could be this enthralled by a sermon. The hour flew by, and I didn't want it to end. After the sermon, the pastor closed his eyes and prayed. Before walking offstage, he invited anyone who wanted prayer for anything to come up to the front of the stage from either side of the auditorium, where people were waiting to pray for them. As the worship band began playing, everyone in the congregation stood and began singing again, songs that were foreign to me.

I had just been moved more than I had ever been before, but I was still uncomfortable in this unfamiliar environment. I stood up along with the rest of the congregation to avoid drawing attention to myself. I considered going over to the side of the auditorium and asking for prayer, but doing so would mean admitting to myself that this all could be real. And I wasn't sure I was ready for the impact such admission would have on my life. For some reason a thought came to me that Colin, who had invited me to church, was probably watching every move I made. So I just stood there frozen, simply too embarrassed to move.

As the music continued, I kept feeling the pull to ask for prayer. I would take one step forward, but then immediately step back. This went on for several minutes. I must have looked ridiculous as I wrestled internally with myself. Finally, I just thought, *You know what, I'm here. I might as well do this.* So I walked down the aisle, to the right side of the auditorium, and went to the nearest person I could find on the prayer team.

I said, "Hi. I'm not a Christian, and I don't know what I believe, but I'm here."

He responded immediately, "Okay, let me pray for you."

He laid his hands on my shoulders and uttered a long and powerful prayer. I don't remember exactly what he prayed, but I remember thinking, *Why does this stranger care about me so much?* There was such a sense of love in his words and tone that I was deeply moved by it. After he finished, I thanked him and made my way back to my seat. The congregation was still standing and singing, then they began lining up to take Communion. But reeling from all the stimuli, and feeling unsteady on my feet, I sat down to let my mind process it all—the sermon, the prayer, the music.

All of a sudden, a giant wave of God's presence came crashing over me. A flood of intense warmth, emotion, and power coursed through me. I didn't understand it at the time, but I now believe it was the Holy Spirit. I had no prior experience with this, no framework for it, and no way of anticipating it, but it was the most penetrating moment I had ever experienced. I was utterly overwhelmed, and I started bawling uncontrollably. It was a kind of weeping that I had never experienced; an extremely deep, retching sob. In a way, it was like an infant's cry, which makes sense considering I had just been born . . . again.

Looking back, I think of Paul's words from so long ago: "[The] gospel came to you not only in word, but also in power and in the Holy Spirit and with full conviction" (1 Thess. 1:5). I was doubled over from the magnitude of it all. Then it happened. I don't know how to describe it other than to say that God revealed himself to me. In that moment, everything became clear: God was real, Jesus was real, the Bible was real, the resurrection was real, heaven was real, hell was real—it was all real. Everything that I had dismissed as a fairy tale was all true. Like Paul, it was as if the scales fell from my eyes and I was able to see. It was as if a curtain had parted and I could finally see the truth. The mysteries of faith were unlocked in that split second. The meaning of my life became absolutely clear. I finally knew where I came from, what I was doing here, and where I was going.

I continued heaving for the next twenty minutes. It honestly felt like the prophet Isaiah's vision of the Lord in the temple:

> The foundations of the thresholds shook at the voice of him who called, and the house was filled with smoke. And I said: "Woe is me! For I am lost; for I am a man of unclean lips . . . for my eyes have seen the King, the LORD of hosts!"
>
> Then one of the seraphim flew to me, having in his hand a burning coal that he had taken with tongs from the

altar. And he touched my mouth and said: "Behold, this has touched your lips; your guilt is taken away, and your sin atoned for." (Isa. 6:4–7)

God revealed his holiness to me, and I saw the utter depth of my sin in light of his holiness. I felt this mix of deep sorrow and incredible joy—sorrow over my sin and joy over meeting Jesus Christ—and gratefulness for everything that meant. In front of a holy God, I was unworthy. But God had mercy on me and took away all my guilt and shame through the blood of Jesus so long ago. My sins were forgiven, and I was reconciled to God through Christ. Every Christian term I had heard over the years to describe this indescribable reality was appropriate: "saved," "born again," "regenerated," "adopted into the family of God," "given eternal life"!

A SECOND DOSE

When the service ended, I collected myself and made my way out to my car. I was in a daze. I don't really remember driving home. *What just happened?*

Back in my apartment I crawled into bed, feeling wiped out by the experience. As I lay there, though, trying to sleep, it happened again. God's presence overwhelmed me, and through his Spirit, God revealed even *more* of himself to me. It was as if the lights in the room brightened so that I could see everything around me more clearly. It felt like gallons of love were being poured into me. I think of Moses in the cleft of the rock as God's glory passed by (Ex. 33:21–23). As John Wesley described it, "I felt my heart strangely warmed."[1]

It's difficult to explain all of what I experienced or understood in that moment, except to say that the Spirit was there with me, drawing me closer to God. I was stunned. I jumped out of bed and began sobbing again, completely blown away by who God was. In the middle of my bedroom, I cried out, "God! You have my life! It's all yours!" I surrendered everything to God right then and there. Then a rush of intense love and peace washed over me, a kind of love and peace I had never experienced before. I was all in.

There was absolutely no turning back now.

BUT WHAT ABOUT DATING GUYS?

After my stunning encounters with God, I knew I could no longer pursue romantic relationships with men. Throughout my life I had been more or less aware of what the Bible had to say on this subject, but my experience brought with it a sense of certainty that being with another man was never God's intention for me. I had finally come to the realization that homosexual behavior was a distortion of God's perfect design for human sexuality and flourishing. Put plainly, I accepted that it was a sin.

Surprisingly, I was perfectly fine with this realization. The complete reversal of my opinions and pursuits in this area worked like this: I had just met the King of the universe! The last thing on my mind was men. To say that every other relationship paled in comparison with my new relationship with Christ would be a massive understatement. How could I hold on to *anything* that didn't bring me closer to Him? My relationship with Christ was the real deal. I knew in my bones that it was what I had been longing for my whole life. It was what I was made for!

I was a new man. Paul's words rang true for me: "If anyone is in Christ, he is a new creation. The old has passed away; behold, the new has come" (2 Cor. 5:17). I *felt* like a new creation. I no longer felt consumed by a desire for men. God's love was more than enough; I didn't need or want anyone else.

My encounter with God didn't happen as a result of a lengthy study. Every day prior to September 20, 2009, I had flat out rejected anything that stood against my identity as a gay man. Years earlier, when I was living in Benedict Canyon with my boyfriend, someone had given me the book *Mere Christianity* by C. S. Lewis. I remembered reading The Chronicles of Narnia by Lewis as a child, so I was curious to know what he had to say about Christianity. The book was interesting enough, but when I got to a chapter where he describes homosexuality as "the perverted desire of a man for a man,"[2] I threw the book across my bedroom, and then into the trash can.

Now I found myself agreeing with Lewis. I never could have imagined that I would change my mind about something so significant to me. However, I realized that it wasn't about simply changing my mind, but about changing my mind *and* heart. I can't explain all the mechanics of this radical transformation. I just know that no one can be in the very presence of the living God and remain the same. Nothing else could have set my life on this new course.

IN THE NICK OF TIME

A curious thing happened in 2008, about a year prior to my conversion to Christianity. I had been living with Daniel, my boyfriend of two years, who was a successful musician in a cool pop band. I looked forward to picking him up from the airport every time he returned from a tour. But this time something felt different. He had just returned from a tour in England and was exhausted from the grueling tour schedule, not to mention the hideously long flight, so I ignored the feeling. As I was driving up La Cienega Boulevard to our apartment, I asked if he wanted to stop and get a cup of coffee at our usual spot on Melrose Avenue. He nodded. I pulled up to the café, scoring a prime parking spot, and was about to get out of the car but noticed he wasn't reaching for his door handle. Something was wrong.

"Are you okay?" I asked.

He didn't respond. Suddenly my heart sank. This was out

of character for someone who was normally so buoyant and cheerful.

I then asked incredulously, "Are we breaking up?"

He looked down, not responding.

I was completely taken aback. Everything had been going so well. I thought we were in love. We hardly ever fought. This was way out of left field. He didn't give any specific reason for wanting to break up, other than to say that he thought it would be best. To this day, I still don't fully understand why.

I restarted the car, and we drove home in silence. Once at the apartment, he promptly packed up his things. Right before he left, we hugged and started crying. Neither of us wanted to let go, as if neither of us wanted this to happen. Then, just like that, it was over. After he left I was numb. Later, when it sank in, I was devastated.

Looking back on that time, I can see God's hand in it. God intervened in that relationship to remove the final obstacle between me and him. Of course, today, I'm exceedingly grateful he did. I see how much he loved me, and how much he wanted me to come to him with nothing in the way.

A NEW LOVE LANGUAGE

Another interesting phenomenon occurred; this time, after my conversion. Before that day, if I ever tried to read the Bible—in my Jesuit Catholic high school religion class, for example—the words seemed dead on the page. I didn't really understand them, and so reading them was boring and tedious. But after my conversion, the words came alive and suddenly the Bible became the most fascinating book in the world. As I read it, the words seemed to jump off the page and began to make sense. It was as if before my conversion the Bible was written in a language I didn't understand, but after my conversion I was fluent in that language.

John Calvin perfectly described what I was experiencing. He said that once the Spirit of God opens a person's eyes, "Scripture exhibits fully as clear evidence of its own truth as white and black things do of their color, or sweet and bitter things do of their taste."[3] I immediately recognized God's voice in the Bible. It was like picking up the phone, hearing the voice on the other end, and knowing it's your mother; or like a baby knowing whether the milk is sour or sweet. You just know. As Jesus said, "My sheep hear my voice, and I know them, and they follow me" (John 10:27).

As I read my Bible, chapter after chapter confirmed exactly what I had experienced that day. Every word resonated in my mind and soul as absolute truth. "The sum of your word is truth" (Ps. 119:160). I couldn't put it down. I wanted to know everything I possibly could about the God I had just met. It was like falling in love and wanting to know everything you can about that person. You want to read their diaries, talk to them for hours, ask them a million questions. I was smitten. But infinitely so.

Not only did I attend church services at Reality LA and their Bible studies with great excitement every week, but I also began to listen to hundreds of sermon podcasts from various pastors who were recommended to me by my new Christian friends. The more I listened, the more I understood the Bible—what it said, what it meant, and how it all fit together. It might sound strange, but I was honestly riveted by these sermons. I was much more interested in listening to sermons than in watching television or movies. In fact, a week after I got saved, I canceled my cable TV subscription. When the AT&T representative asked me why I was canceling, I responded, "It's a distraction I don't need." I had no interest in anything that wasn't about God. I had been starved of the truth for too long. I also canceled my lifelong subscription to the *New Yorker*, which I used to read religiously every week. The articles that once seemed so important, erudite, and deep for all those years now felt trivial, foolish, and shallow.

For at least fifteen years I had listened to NPR all day, every day. Every morning after waking, I would go right to the kitchen and make coffee, and as soon as I put the water on to boil, I would turn to the public radio station, KCRW. I'd listen to the music programs all morning, the news programs all afternoon, and then more music at night. But now, that station had zero appeal to me. I just wanted to hear truth all day long and be immersed in the Bible, sermons, and worship music.

I also read countless theological books: Augustine's *Confessions*, John Bunyan's *The Pilgrim's Progress*, Dietrich Bonhoeffer's *The Cost of Discipleship*, C. S. Lewis's entire oeuvre (including *Mere Christianity*, only this time I didn't throw it across the room), and others. I couldn't get enough of the truth. The more I learned about God, the more I wanted to know. I was interested only in eternal things. "Set your minds on things that are above, not on things that are on earth" (Col. 3:2).

COMING OUT:
THE SECOND TIME AROUND

It took some time for me to recover from the shock of my conversion. I didn't tell anyone for a couple of weeks, then slowly, I began emailing members of my family. Being new to my faith, I spaced out the emails so I wouldn't get overwhelmed with responses. The divine Physician had me in an incubator, protecting me and giving me time to grow and acclimate to my new life. I wasn't quite ready for any abrupt phone calls from excited family members; all seven of my siblings and both of my parents have been strong Christians for many years. (God had crazy grace on my entire family!) When the phone calls did start coming in, there was unbelievable excitement and many tears on both ends of the line. My family was beside themselves with joy. The prodigal son was home at last! The feeling of alienation I always felt when I was with them (mostly self-inflicted) vanished upon my conversion. I no longer felt like they were the enemy. I no longer felt estranged from them because of who I was. And I no longer felt misunderstood. We were finally on the same page.

Other things changed as well. I no longer cared about making my mark on this world. I no longer cared about people's opinions of me. I was no longer afraid of death. All that stuff just melted away. I felt so free! "For freedom Christ has set us free" (Gal. 5:1). I also realized what a fool I had been. All those years I thought I was so wise, while rejecting the very foundation of wisdom. "The fear of the LORD is the beginning of wisdom" (Prov. 9:10). Now I was truly wise and could see that all my life pursuits and grand accomplishments came from my foolish rejection of God.

What can be known about God is plain to them, because God has shown it to them. For his invisible attributes, namely, his eternal power and divine nature, have been clearly perceived, ever since the creation of the world, in the things that have been made. So they are without excuse. For although they knew God, they did not honor him as God or give thanks to him, but they became futile in their thinking, and their foolish hearts were darkened. Claiming to be wise, they became fools, and exchanged the glory of the immortal God for images resembling mortal man and birds and animals and creeping things.

Therefore God gave them up in the lusts of their hearts to impurity, to the dishonoring of their bodies among themselves, because they exchanged the truth about God for a lie and worshiped and served the creature rather than the Creator, who is blessed forever! Amen. (Rom. 1:19–25)

I was finally seeing the wisdom of the Scriptures, the very thing I had once considered foolish.

The word of the cross is folly to those who are perishing, but to us who are being saved it is the power of God. For it is written,

> "I will destroy the wisdom of the wise,
>> and the discernment of the discerning I will
>> thwart."

Where is the one who is wise? Where is the scribe? Where is the debater of this age? Has not God made foolish the wisdom of the world? For since, in the wisdom of God, the world did not know God through wisdom, it pleased God through the folly of what we preach to save those who believe. (1 Cor. 1:18–21)

Let no one deceive himself. If anyone among you thinks that he is wise in this age, let him become a fool that he may become wise. For the wisdom of this world is folly with God. (1 Cor. 3:18–19)

I had to become a fool before I could become wise. And for the first time in my life, I was more than happy to be so.

THREE

CHILDHOOD:
THE CONFLICT BEGINS

I began to wonder what had led me to identify as a gay man. Hearing the gospel that day and being transformed by the Holy Spirit unraveled that false identity in a heartbeat, but it was a long and colorful road before that joyous day in 2009.

My childhood was by all accounts idyllic, at least on paper. I was the youngest of eight children in a devout Catholic family, with six boys and two girls. I was born and raised in Dallas, Texas, with parents who were committed, for better or worse, to their vows of marriage. It wasn't always an easy marriage, as I guess no marriage is. They had their fair share of dramatic and volatile "George and Martha" moments (from *Who's Afraid of Virginia Woolf?*), but stuck it out until the bitter end. They died six months apart: my dad in the summer of 2015, and my mother in January of 2016.

The appropriately large house I grew up in was in the affluent Preston Hollow area of town. The Catholic elementary school and the elite all-boys Jesuit preparatory high school I attended were right next door to each other in a desirable part of town, only a couple of miles from our house. My father was a criminal defense attorney, and my mother was a stay-at-home, beauty-parlor mom who required occasional valium (think Don and Betty Draper from *Mad Men*). We had two live-in maids and, at one point, a black Cadillac limousine. (It was Dallas, after all!) My five brothers, two sisters, and I kept the house in a constant state of frenetic activity. We never had a dull moment. This chaos was normal to me because it was all I knew.

My father's old-school, no-nonsense approach to discipline kept us in line. We were well aware of where the boundaries lay, and no one dared cross them—that is, until someone did. He was good at providing a safe, orderly home, but was more or less emotionally unavailable. His work schedule was intense and demanding, and by the time he got home, he didn't have much energy left to engage with eight small, needy children. He was unflappable, though, and didn't seem at all affected by the nonstop circus swirling around him. He had a sturdier constitution than my mother, who didn't adapt to the chaos quite as well; her nerves were frayed more often than not.

When I think of my mother, I think of a giant ball of unbridled emotion and unconditional love. I could go to her with *anything* without fear of judgment. We always had a very open, honest, and easy relationship. I could do no wrong in her eyes. My relationship with my father, on the other hand, was more formal. His imposing, alpha male disposition intimidated me. I rarely felt comfortable talking with him about deeper, emotional issues. He was kind enough, but our interactions were usually brief and superficial. It felt like his love needed to be earned in one way or another, and was always just out of reach. But he created a stable, secure environment to grow up in, so who was I to complain?

I took it all in stride, both amused and perplexed by this mass of people I called family.

FIRST BRUSH WITH PORNOGRAPHY

My brother Peter and I were only eleven months apart, and we were inseparable. We did everything together: discovered the wonders of fire when we set part of the neighbor's front lawn ablaze, learned cool tricks on the diving board, built forts, and so on. When we were very young (eight or nine years old), a neighbor kid invited us to come over while his parents were away and sneak a peek at his father's stash of *Playboy* magazines. Peter and I eagerly accepted and headed up the street to his house. Our friend led us back to his parents' bedroom, where the magazines were hidden (not too successfully), and pulled out a large stack from under the bed. We each grabbed one and began furiously flipping through the pages, gawking at the images of semi-nude women.

This was the first time I had ever seen anything like this. A rush of adrenaline immediately coursed through my body. I had never felt this kind of excitement and was utterly entranced by and drawn to the women in the pictures. I clearly remember this moment as if it happened yesterday, and from this experience I know that my first sexual desires were directed toward women.

This experience awakened in me something I wasn't even aware of. The way my sexual energy was stirred up (through pornography) led to me having an unhealthy understanding of sexuality. I ended up feeling desire for my male friends from the neighborhood and from school, because I had nowhere else to place these newfound, sexual desires; they were the only ones I was around. At that young age, we typically hang out with friends of the same sex. I believe this was the genesis of my developing attractions to guys instead of girls, although, at the time, I didn't fully comprehend the emotions I was feeling.

NIGHT TERROR

A couple of years later, when I was ten years old, I was at the home of a good friend of mine, Philip, for a sleepover. What happened there would become one of the most scarring moments of my life.

Back then, sleepovers were common among my friends, and I had spent the night at Philip's house several times before this particular night. After a long day of activities and dinner with his family, Philip and I each took a bath before bedtime, and as usual, I slept in the guest room. But in the middle of the night I awoke to a strange sensation I had never experienced before: Philip's father was performing oral sex on me. I could smell alcohol on his breath, and I was terrified. I was stock-still, pretending to be asleep, for fear of angering him. I was convinced that if he knew I was awake he would stab me with a knife. (I'm not sure why my mind conjured such a specific image.) After a few minutes, he got up and left the room.

My mind was racing. I didn't know what to do or think. A few minutes later, when he came back, I had turned over on my stomach. Again, I pretended to be asleep. But when he grabbed my side with both hands and tried to turn me over, I resisted. He tried several more times, but I continued to resist. I'm not sure how I mustered the courage—it was risky—but I refused to let him do that to me again. He finally left.

When he came back a third time, I was sitting up, fully awake. I was done pretending. He kind of stuttered a bit and asked if I needed a fan (a lame excuse for being in the room). When I said an emphatic no, he left for good. Somehow I was able to sleep through the rest of the night.

The next morning, soon after I woke up, my mother arrived to get me. On my way out, I crossed paths with Philip's father. When I glanced at him, a creepy grin came over his face. It stirred up a combination of fear and anger in me, and I quickly averted my gaze. I never went back to that house again.

I decided never to tell my parents about the incident. I knew that if my dad found out he probably would have murdered the guy, or had him murdered, and I didn't want that heavy burden on me. I couldn't fathom the idea of my father going to prison and leaving my mother without a husband and all of us without a father. And, of course, the shame of it all was too much. I didn't want to be seen as damaged goods by my family and friends. I did, however, tell my friend Johnny, whom I had known since we were little. Our families were also close. By telling him, I no longer felt as if I was bottling it up in some unhealthy, dangerous way. I thought, *At least I'd told someone, right?*

Many years later, when I was in my thirties, my parents found out. Unbeknownst to me, Johnny had told my brother Peter about the incident soon after I'd told him. And, probably in an effort to help my parents understand why I was gay, Peter told them what had happened. At the time I was furious at Peter, because I didn't think that experience had any impact on my sexual identity. I refused to accept that my proud, gay identity was somehow tied to a disturbing and disgusting experience.

I remember a phone conversation I had with my father, telling him that I was unequivocally *born* gay. But now I understand how that traumatic night had enormously impacted my sexuality. I'm not saying that everyone who is sexually molested as a child winds up being gay. I know men and women who were molested as children and went on to live heterosexual lives. I'm just saying that, in my case, having already waded in the waters of same-sex attraction before I was sexually molested—and before I saw myself as gay—the experience somehow locked those feelings into place in an irreparable way. Maybe there was some kind of genetic predisposition. I don't know. I also don't know the exact calculus on how that night bent my desire toward men in a more permanent way. But I am certain, as I look back on that night and ponder, it did affect my same-sex attraction.

Years later, when I was in Dallas for the holidays, my father and I had dinner. I brought up the subject of the molestation and explained what had happened that night. I then asked him what he would have done if I had told him when it happened. He said he would have given Philip's father two options: turn himself in or. . . . I knew what he meant, even though he didn't say the words; just what I had feared. I recently discovered that Philip's father died in 1991.

SAME-SEX ATTRACTION BLOOMS

In sixth and seventh grades, I became increasingly aware that I was attracted to the same sex. It didn't trouble me that much at first. I just thought the feelings were temporary and would eventually go away, that I was going through some sort of a phase that lots of boys go through. *I've heard about this kind of thing in England. Yeah, that's what it is.*

Of course, I kept silent about these unwanted feelings. I knew that if word got out I would be ostracized. I also knew the very clear message from my family, my religion, and the conservative culture around me: these feelings were wrong and abnormal. That belief suited me fine at the time, as I did not *want* to be attracted to other guys. So I kept my feelings hidden.

As time went on, however, the feelings grew stronger, and I started to become attracted to the guys in my class. Then I learned that my friend Johnny was experiencing same-sex attraction as well, as was another friend we'd had known since kindergarten, Max. The three of us were close enough to be very open with one another about the strange but exciting feelings we were having. Johnny and Max were much more zealous when it came to their attraction to guys and were not afraid to explore their sexuality. They urged me to come along with them and strongly encouraged me to explore my desires. But we kept all this hidden; no one was the wiser, not our classmates, teachers, or families.

Looking back, I can see that between Philip's father and my two close friends, I didn't have a chance. The cards were stacked against me turning out heterosexual. I believe my sexuality could have developed differently had I been protected from those experiences. I may have turned out straight if my early years had been saturated in healthy relationships. I'll never know. At the time, though, I was just happy to have friends like Johnny and Max. These two guys provided a community of support for me. They helped me feel like I wasn't the only boy in the world going through this, and I appreciated having them to confide in.

Meanwhile, I had a whole other group of friends. I was a very social kid and popular among my schoolmates. I went steady with several girls in my class, mostly because I liked the social interaction and the affirmation of my guy friends. But that part of my life was almost like a game to me. I was drawn to the excitement and satisfaction of winning them over, but had no real attraction to the girls I dated.

This double life taught me how to compartmentalize, and I learned to live with these two very different lives easily. My secret was safe.

HIGH SCHOOL

My same-sex attraction continued as I moved from my coed elementary school to my all-boys Jesuit high school. My double life continued as well, and I dated girls knowing full well that I was actually attracted to boys. But again, dating was fun socially. I was popular in high school. I had lots of Jesuit friends and never lacked invitations to the many dances and debutante balls at the two main all-girls schools: Ursuline Academy and Hockaday. I was in demand, so keeping my same-sex attraction under wraps seemed that much more important; there was more at stake and more to lose. If any of my guy friends found out I would have been immediately cast out, so I was determined to keep my secret safe. But as each year passed, I became acutely aware of my inner conflict. I began to internally identify more and more as gay and felt trapped, and I longed to be free.

I was getting straight A's in high school, so my parents didn't bother me much. I was also the youngest of eight kids, which meant that by the time they got to me, they were pretty much hands-off. My parents had already been put through the wringer by some of my more rebellious older siblings, so they were just happy to see me put on my blue blazer and striped tie every morning and make it to school on time. I flew under their radar by getting good grades and not causing trouble. As far as my parents were concerned, I was a hassle-free, delightful son. Unlike my siblings, I never had a curfew, or any other restrictions for that matter.

Things were good, as long as I did well in school and faithfully performed my weekly Catholic duties during Communion and confession. Growing up, I assented to my parents' faith in an effort to please them. I wanted their approval and knew this was one of the most important ways to get it. "Just keep your head down and go through the motions" was my motto. I didn't feel a personal connection to God. He just wasn't a reality in my daily life. And the more I dove into my developing sexual identity, the less interest I had in him.

During my junior year of high school, I established a very close friendship with a fellow student named Jack, who was also experiencing same-sex attraction. We each kind of knew the other was in the same boat, but we never spoke about the giant pink elephant in the room. It was during this time that I first stepped into a wonderfully chic nightclub: the infamous Starck Club, designed by the legendary French designer Philippe Starck.

I'm not sure how Jack and I got in at the tender age of fifteen, but the stylish doorman not only let us in, he also waived the expensive cover charge. When I crossed the threshold, walking past the opulent black-lacquered doors, I entered a world that was totally new to me. As I strolled around the neoclassical space, with its all-white couches and chairs divided in sections by billowing white curtains, and brilliant New Wave music of Pet Shop Boys and New Order blasting, I witnessed a wild mix of humanity: drag queens, gay guys, straight business dudes, and beautiful and fashionable women. As I took in the atmosphere, I felt a sense of community. These were my kind of people, and this was my kind of place. I spent many nights there over the following years.

That first visit to the Starck Club dramatically changed my friendship with Jack. My childhood friends Max and Johnny were on the periphery of my life by this point, but Max happened to be there that night as well. The troublemaker that he was, he devised a plan to get Jack and me to admit to each other that we were attracted to guys. He pulled Jack aside and told him my secret and that I desperately wanted to tell him. He then found me across the club and told me Jack's secret and that he desperately wanted to tell me. Minutes later, I saw Jack walking toward me with a sort of embarrassed smile on his face. I smiled back. Then we hugged each other, and that was that. We officially came out to each other.

After this pivotal moment, things progressed rapidly. I finally had a best friend in high school with whom I could share my innermost secrets. And soon we began going to gay bars together in the forbidden and frowned-upon Cedar Springs part of town. I had found a world where *everyone* was like me, and I coveted this deep sense of belonging. I didn't have to hide my feelings at all in this open-minded, liberated atmosphere. The truth was out, and no one seemed to care. I felt free at last.

Although my desires for men were very real at that time, I still thought of them as temporary, not as a long-term, permanent emotion. In the back of my mind I always assumed that eventually these attractions would go away, and I would marry a woman and have a traditional family. I didn't really worry too much about it, thinking I'd move on when my desires changed. For the moment, though, I was content to just go with my feelings, excited by all the new discoveries I was making and the adventures I was going on. I focused on enjoying the here and now.

High school was one of the best periods of my life. And leading a double life only added to the excitement. Because of my atypical sexuality, I was able to see life through a different lens, one that intrigued me. I almost felt lucky to have this unique perspective on life. Being a part of this secret club made me feel special, more complex and interesting, so much so that I began to feel contempt for the conventional. I wanted something extraordinary and exhilarating, and I was living it. The future looked bright.

FOUR

COLLEGE YEARS: GOD IS DEAD

When I went away to college, I wasn't fully out of the closet. I still had one foot in and one foot out, as I continued to wrestle with the idea of homosexuality as a permanent part of my life. At the time, there was a stigma attached to being gay, and I was fine with keeping things quiet. College was a whole new place with new people, and even though the school I attended was a very progressive liberal arts school, I didn't feel comfortable exposing this part of myself yet. I wasn't ready to hang a rainbow flag in my dorm room or interested in making some big statement. I just wanted to fit in. I had years of practice staying under the radar, and it helped me in this new environment.

I was premed in college, mostly because I excelled in math and science in high school and figured I might as well use that to my advantage careerwise. Pursuing a major that had as its prerequisites courses that came easy to me seemed like the natural choice. Growing up in my community in Dallas, the professional options were tacitly understood to be limited to doctor, lawyer, or businessperson. That's it. The idea of making a career out of some creative interest or passion was completely foreign. Being a doctor would bring security and wealth, not to mention respect from my family and community, so why not? My primary goal, therefore, was to make the best grades possible in my rigorous science and math classes. And that's exactly what I did. I avoided distractions on campus and kept my eye on the prize.

At the beginning of my freshman year, I met a sophomore, Martin, who was also attracted to guys and lived in my dorm. We became fast friends. This burgeoning friendship was similar to the relationship I had with Jack in high school. Once again, both of us knew the other was gay (although we didn't use that label, at least not yet), but neither of us mentioned it. As the semester progressed, we grew closer and closer. Then one day in his dorm room, while listening to the Smiths on his record player, we came out to each other.

Martin and I had similar tastes in music, art, humor, and nice restaurants. He would come upstairs to my dorm room every morning to get me before going to breakfast. We co-deejayed a weekly dance party on campus called "New Music Mondays." We hung out in his room when our homework was done. We chatted about life, literature, and love. And again, I had a confidant to share all my secret feelings with.

BROMANCE-ISH

In the winter, things shifted. Martin decided that it was time for him to come out of the closet officially as a gay man. I was horrified. I was in no way ready to come out (or even really to admit that I was gay), but knew that if he did, I would get dragged out with him. I made it very clear to him that I wasn't ready to do the same and urged him to wait, but his mind was made up. His decision to be out loud and proud put a major wrench in our friendship. I feared the stigma attached to coming out and felt it was way too soon in my college career to risk this kind of public disclosure. The last thing I wanted was to become the object of the whispers and murmurs of other students on campus. I quickly began distancing myself from Martin. He was deeply hurt by this, but he left me no other choice.

Meanwhile, I was developing a brand-new friendship with a fellow classmate named Tommy. We became best friends very quickly, which hurt Martin even more. I developed a huge crush on Tommy, but there was only one problem: he was straight. That didn't stop us from having an intense emotional affair, however, similar to those found in the classic Oxbridge schoolmate romances. We were like Charles and Sebastian in Evelyn Waugh's *Brideshead Revisited*; I was Sebastian (without the drinking problem), and Tommy was Charles. At this point, Martin and I were cordial, but we barely hung out. When we ran into each other on campus, our conversations were brief and strained. My interest now lay elsewhere.

I never told Tommy that I was attracted to guys, but it was pretty clear to him. Regardless, we spent all our free time together, practically attached at the hip. We even pledged a fraternity together. But after a few weeks, I realized my grades would suffer if I continued with the grueling and time-consuming obligations of a pledge. The massive amount of time and work needed to maintain my high GPA was all I could handle, so I quit, while Tommy stuck with it. My decision to leave the fraternity fractured our relationship irreparably. I think he felt a little betrayed by my backing out, and I felt as if he had moved on to a new network of friends.

As Tommy spent more and more time with his fraternity brothers, I gradually understood that things would never be the same. Our relationship couldn't withstand the damage done by my choice to exit fraternity life. It was a sad time for both of us. Soon after the dissolution of our friendship, Martin came back into my life. We didn't really address the interruption of the Tommy epoch and simply resumed where we had left off. But we were separated again because of his move to Freiburg, Germany, for his junior-year-abroad study program.

VIENNA CALLING

A year later, when Martin returned from Germany, I headed to Vienna for my own junior year abroad. We were like two ships (or planes) in the night. Vienna had me at *Grüß Gott!* It was my first time in Europe, and my first time traveling outside the United States. I immediately took to this grand European capital, with its magnificent baroque architecture and legendary *Sachertorte*. This city, known for Mozart, Freud, and Klimt, was just the right place for me. I was overwhelmed by the city's beauty and grandeur and mesmerized by its foreignness. But oddly enough, I felt very much at home, even though my German was sketchy at best. I could roam the streets for hours, marveling at the sheer beauty.

Of course, a new school meant all new friends, and as usual I made them quickly. But this time I had no one to confide in regarding my sexuality. (The irony is that one of my two roommates in our grand, eighteenth-century apartment in the fourth district of the city was gay, but I had no idea at the time. I only found out years later.) I kept my sexual proclivities under wraps, until one day a classmate called it into question. A girl asked me quite bluntly if I was gay, and I immediately denied it. She didn't seem convinced, but she didn't pursue it any further. The incident unnerved me a bit, but no one else questioned my sexuality, and I was able to successfully remain in the closet the rest of my time in Vienna.

My senior year of college was dedicated mostly to schoolwork and preparing for the MCAT (medical college admission test). I didn't have time for socializing, and I chose to remain closeted. My logic was that it would be less scandalous to come out after graduation. The intense social scrutiny inherent in college life and the burden of intimacy that permeated a small liberal arts college made coming out too risky. I thought I would better enjoy the emancipation in the unfettered life of the real world that comes with anonymity. So I pushed through my senior year without initiating what I knew would become an overblown, emotional event.

My overall experience in college in regard to God was remarkable: I entered college a vague theist but left a staunch atheist. I was very much indoctrinated into the prevailing secular humanist worldview that dominated campus life. Most of my professors (if not all) were, to my knowledge, atheists. God was *never* discussed, and Christians were seen as backward and ignorant. My classmates didn't seem to have any interest in God; I don't think I knew a single Christian on campus. And, as far as I was aware, there were no Christian groups on campus either. I was slowly but surely pulled away from any notion that God existed, and certainly not a God who had any relevance in life. The character of Charles in *Brideshead Revisited* quite nicely summed up my feelings regarding religion at the time:

The view implicit in my education was that the basic narrative of Christianity had long been exposed as a myth, and that opinion was now divided as to whether its ethical teaching was of present value, a division in which the main weight went against it: religion was a hobby which some people professed and others did not; at best it was slightly ornamental, at worst it was the providence of "complexes" and "inhibitions"—catchwords of the decade—and of the intolerance, hypocrisy, and sheer stupidity attributed to it for centuries. No one had ever suggested to me that these quaint observances expressed a coherent philosophic system and intransigent historical claims; nor, had they done so, would I have been much interested.[1]

This all suited me just fine. I was happy to be free of any constraints that belief in God would place on me. I was not ready for such a yoke. I had more pressing and exciting matters at hand: my auspicious future, my prestigious career, and my search for love.

FIVE

FROM TOKYO
WITH LOVE

I did relatively well on the MCAT, but by the time I got my results back, my interest in medical school began to wane. I started to question whether I *really* want to become a doctor. As I mentioned, my motives for choosing premed in college were no deeper than marrying my natural aptitude in math and science with my desire to be a well-respected professional. It wasn't until my senior year that I began to contemplate what it would truly mean to be a doctor. I thought about the real-life, day-to-day work, and realized I had no interest.

I had been so buried in my studies that I didn't stop to notice that I was an artist at heart. I had taken several studio art classes as electives because that was what I enjoyed doing. And, growing up, I had always been drawn to art films, the Dallas Opera, and the Dallas Museum of Art. They were the kinds of things that interested me.

But a profession in the arts was simply unheard of among my family and friends. My parents certainly never encouraged me in any artistic pursuits. And my siblings were just as oblivious to my sensibilities as my parents. I remember one day watching *Who's Afraid of Virginia Woolf?* on video for the umpteenth time, when my sister, as she was walking by the living room, said dismissively, "Oh, isn't this that movie about two people fighting?" I ignored her, but I was livid. I thought, *What? It's so much more than that! Don't you get it?* I believe I always had a sensitive, artistic soul. Now I just had to figure out how to earn a living in the arts.

When I thought about what I wanted to do with my time and energy for the rest of my life, I kept coming back to some sort of creative endeavor. Writing? Acting? Designing? I wasn't sure. But I knew that a conventional path wasn't for me. I wanted to mine the creative ore deep in my soul that had gone untouched my whole life. I wanted to do something big. I wanted to make my mark on this world. But I didn't know where to begin. This epiphany was quite upsetting, since I had just poured four years of blood, sweat, and tears trying to get into medical school. I was in a panic about my future and had no idea what to do.

TOKYO

My friend Martin was also going through a postcollege creative crisis of his own. He had considered law school, and at the time was working as an assistant at a law firm in Houston, but he wasn't sure it was a good fit for him. He had some interest in becoming a chef but needed time to think it through. He suggested taking a year off to evaluate our options.

His idea was to move to Tokyo to teach English, which at that time was a quite lucrative endeavor; Americans in particular were in high demand for these positions in Japan. This interlude would give both of us time to figure things out, with the added bonus of an exciting adventure in a far-off land. It would also mean living in one of the coolest cities in the world, with easy money and new experiences. What could be better? After giving the idea some thought, I agreed it was the perfect solution to our dilemma. I could put off the real world for a year or so, using the time to make a more thoughtful decision about the future. So, soon after my graduation, Martin and I packed our bags and flew to Japan.

We arrived in Tokyo with little money and no job prospects. But the very next day, we were hired to teach English at a popular English school with branches all over Tokyo. We also found an apartment that same week. I was surprised how quickly and easily things were working out. Tokyo was a fascinating, bustling place, and each day was an exciting new adventure as we explored and experienced this vast, unending city, with its extreme mass of people (I had never seen so many people in my life!) and breathtaking explosion of neon lights. This was my home for now, and I loved it.

Martin and I quickly found what would become our favorite gay bar, Kinsmen, in the Shinjuku Ni-chōme district of Tokyo. The clientele was a mix of Japanese men and others from all over the world. It had an international vibe, with many different languages spoken, an interesting mix of people, and great music. It was like Paris of the 1920s, but in 1990s Tokyo.

Now that I was so far from home and reality, I finally felt free to express my sexuality, which was ironic, considering that homosexuality was very much a taboo in Japanese culture back then. Japan lagged behind the United States by a couple of decades in terms of its social acceptance of homosexuality. In this giant metropolis of 11 million people, there were only a handful of gay bars, and most of them were underground. Almost all the Japanese men I met at Kinsmen were closeted and living deeply secret double lives, since they would have been disowned by their families if they were ever found out. A Japanese guy I befriended told me that if he told his parents, it would bring deep shame upon the family. And he would not only be risking their rejection but also his job, because Japanese "salarymen," as they were called, were expected to be straight. Being openly gay in Japan wasn't an option in the business world, or any other part of society for that matter.

But despite Japan's "backwardness" on this issue, and the country's exceedingly rigid and often frustrating cultural norms, I was able to come into my own more than ever as a gay man. I was finally comfortable with that label.

During this time, I thought a lot about the future. I knew I was better suited for a creative career, but I had doubts about whether that was possible. Moreover, it seemed like a huge risk. What if I spent years pursuing a career in the arts, only to find out that I wasn't any good? I was afraid of failing and wasting valuable time that I could have spent pursuing a steadier, more solid career path. So I kept thinking in terms of conventional professions and decided to apply to law school. I thought maybe the best way to go about finding my path was to rule things out. I spent several months studying on my own for the LSAT and took the exam in Tokyo of all places. Months later I got my test results and was shocked that I had done so well. I wondered, *Oh no, now what? Maybe I'm supposed to go to law school?*

I obviously had serious doubts that law school was the answer, but I applied anyway just as a backup plan and was accepted to a couple of top schools. I even enrolled in one of them! But what about all that talk of becoming an artist?

LISA COMES TO JAPAN

A few months into my year in Tokyo, a close friend from home, Lisa, called and said that she wanted to move there. She was going through a crisis of her own after leaving a volatile and unhealthy relationship with a boyfriend, and Tokyo seemed like a good way to escape. It was as far away as she could get from this guy. She arrived a few weeks later and moved in with Martin and me. Our studio apartment was tiny, and although Martin bristled in the beginning, he soon succumbed to her deeply charming and wildly entertaining personality. So there we were, three Americans stuffed into a pocket-size Tokyo apartment.

Lisa loved our regular hangout spot, Kinsmen, and she and I enjoyed more than our share of debauched nights together. One night we went out clubbing in the hip district of Roppongi and thought it would be a good idea to steal several bottles of liquor from the bar at one of the clubs, hiding them in our coats, then give them to a bartender at another club nearby and have him make us free drinks with our spoils. The guy was confused but poured us the drinks anyway. Later that night, we hopped on my motor scooter and headed home. (I ended up buying a scooter in Tokyo because the trains and subways stopped at 12:30 a.m., and I always wanted to stay out later. Tokyo was so giant and sprawling that taking a cab cost a small fortune.) But on the way I spotted a police car and freaked out, because having another person on the back of a one-seater scooter was illegal in Japan. I yelled at Lisa to get off, and she leaped off before I had a chance to fully stop. She hit the pavement and slid down an alleyway, out of sight. Fortunately, she was okay; just a minor scrape or two. I think her blood alcohol level softened the landing. The policeman was none the wiser.

FALLING IN LOVE

A month or two later, Lisa's friend Adam arrived in Tokyo for a visit. He was one of the two thousand volunteer workers who helped install the enormous art project *The Umbrellas*, by the famed artist Christo, all across Japan. He was from Dallas and a fine arts student at the University of Texas at Austin.

The night he arrived, the three of us met him at Ebisu Station and then headed to our favorite restaurant, Ninniku-ya, located in the youthful and fashionable part of Tokyo called Shibuya. I wasn't that impressed with Adam during our initial interaction at the train station. He had an interesting look, but a matinee idol he was not. But my perception of him gradually changed as the night wore on. He was quite charming, funny, and engaging. I was intrigued, but still not sold in terms of viewing him in any sort of romantic way.

While Adam stayed with us for several days (four Americans in a tiny Japanese apartment!), he and I began taking an interest in each other, and our conversations took a flirtatious turn. The night before he was to leave, he said he was going to the roof of our building to smoke and asked me to come with him. I gladly accepted. We ended up chatting and kissing all night up on that roof. A spark ignited between us that night. But I thought it would remain just a spark, because he was leaving the next day and I would never see him again. I was wrong.

After Adam left, I returned to my normal routine. I didn't really miss him because we had known each other for only a few days. He quickly became a distant memory—that is, until about a month later, when he called our apartment (this was before cell phones). I picked up the phone, and when I heard his voice I assumed he was calling to talk to Lisa, but he never asked for her. We talked for almost an hour. After I hung up, I was struck by the feelings I had on the rooftop. He stirred up a sense of longing in me, and I couldn't stop wondering, *Did I really like this guy? If I did, does it matter? We probably won't ever live in the same city, so what's the point? But what about the butterflies in my stomach? Ugh. I'm going out for sushi.*

Months later, my Japan epoch was over. I became restless. I felt I had done everything there was to do in Tokyo and needed a change. I was also growing weary of the repressed, group-oriented, honor/shame Japanese culture. I missed the bold, American self-expression. I very rarely met a Japanese person who expressed a strong personal opinion of any kind, and I longed to be around people who weren't afraid to be themselves, voice their opinion, or say what they meant. I missed Western individualism, American pop culture, and hip-hop music! So, after being in Tokyo for almost a year, I decided to move back to Dallas.

A LOVE THAT DARES SPEAK ITS NAME

I arrived home in December, a week or so before Christmas. My parents' house felt like the Versailles compared to the Lilliputian hovel I had been living in for the past year. I felt like ballroom dancing in our living room! I delighted in this large and luxurious atmosphere. I could breathe. It's amazing how adaptable we human beings can be, and how easily we can take things for granted.

The first day I was home, my friend James called, saying he was excited that I was back in town and wanted to stop by. I had learned from Lisa that Adam and James were close friends from high school. What I didn't know, though, was that James would be bringing over a special guest: none other than Adam himself. When I opened the door, I was surprised and delighted to see Adam standing there with a coy grin on his face. I didn't even know he had come home from Austin for Christmas break. When I saw him standing there at my front door on that cold winter night, my heart melted. I was in love.

I was surprised by my reaction. I really didn't think I would ever see him again and had been perfectly fine with that. But I realized then how much I did miss him. We immediately began dating, and soon after officially became boyfriends. This was the first time in my life I had ever been in love. It was an overwhelming feeling that filled me with excitement and joy. This was it. He was the one. Wow. I had read Russian novels about all-consuming love but had never experienced it. I now understood what made Anna Karenina and Madame Bovary tick. *Madame Bovary c'est moi, indeed!*

One result of this new and profound emotion was a stronger sense of my identity as a gay man. This sealed the deal. I am what I am! (I'm alluding, of course, to the Broadway musical *La Cage aux Folles*, not to the book of Exodus.) It empowered me to come out of the closet to everyone, without any reticence whatsoever.

While I was in Tokyo, one of my sisters, Rachel, had written me a letter (yes, this was before email) in which she asked me straight-out if I was gay. Apparently, she'd had her suspicions for a while. I was surprised by the letter but decided to tell the truth. I ended up writing her a lengthy missive elucidating every aspect of what it meant to be gay, personally, socially, politically, biologically, and even economically. At the end of my letter, I urged her not to tell our parents, that I would tell them in person when I got home. But, unbeknownst to me, upon receiving my letter, she promptly told the entire family, completely ignoring my request for discretion.

So, when I returned from Japan, everyone already knew my long-hidden secret, which was just fine by me. I had finally become comfortable in my gay skin, and since Rachel had spilled the beans, I was off the hook from having to do it myself. I was gay, Adam was my boyfriend, and I was proud of it. They just needed to get over it. At that point I had no patience for anyone who was hung up about homosexuality. "Get on board or get out of the way" was my motto. In retrospect, I see that my position was quite unfair. I had years and years to get comfortable with my identity, but I expected my family to get comfortable with it immediately. Not cool.

One night during the holidays, I was in the kitchen making something to eat, while my sweet mother was sitting at the table smoking a cigarette and sipping coffee (her two chief occupations), when she suddenly burst into tears. As soon as I noticed she was crying, I of course knew why. This was the moment all mothers and their gay sons dread: I was about to confirm my mother's biggest fear. She had already heard the news from my sister, but had now finally mustered the courage to ask me directly.

Through her tears, she managed to mutter, "I know you're a homosexual . . ."

I just nodded. But as more tears streamed down her face, I tried to comfort her and said, "Mom, don't worry . . . it's okay . . . it's not a big deal . . . everything will be fine." I tried to assure her that it was nobody's fault, that this was who I was, that I'd always been this way.

Once she cried it out, she seemed better. I'll never forget how gentle and loving she was about it. She was just genuinely concerned about me.

I had a similar interaction with my father a few days later, but without the tears and cigarettes. One day we arrived home at the same time, and he pulled up right behind me in the driveway. As I was heading inside, he got out of his car and stopped me.

He, too, was gentle with me. He asked, "Your mother told me everything. Are you angry at me for not being a better father?"

I told him he was a great father (not entirely true) and that my sexuality had nothing to do with him.

He told me he loved me, and that was it.

Both my parents seemed to be semi-okay with it. There were no dramatic scenes, no pleas for repentance, no kicking me out of the house. They took it in stride. I don't think they had the energy to wrestle with me on this issue, and just stayed out of my business. I was their eighth child, after all. There was soon a "don't ask, don't tell" policy in the house regarding my love life.

Adam and I continued our relationship, spending every moment we could together. This love thing was a new experience for both of us, and we were on cloud ten. But then the holidays came to an end, and Adam had to go back to Austin to finish his junior year. Love, interrupted. We knew the long-distance factor would present some difficulties, but nothing we couldn't overcome. I would drive down to Austin, which was only three hours (if you were willing to risk life and limb), as often as I could, or he would come up to Dallas whenever possible.

I was still unsure of my career direction, but since this new relationship was taking up most of my emotional energy, my career seemed secondary. Law school was still on the table, but I began considering the idea of moving to Los Angeles to try my luck at acting and writing. I knew it was crazy. I think I had always secretly wanted to give it a shot but had been too afraid. My relationship with Adam emboldened me, not only to come out of the closet but also to pursue my dreams. I now had a stronger sense of self, and with Adam by my side, I felt I could achieve anything. The sky was the limit!

In my mind, the plan was to wait until Adam graduated from college in a year and a half, then move to Los Angeles together. But I'm not sure I ever explicitly voiced this plan to him. He knew I wanted to move to Los Angeles, but the details were never discussed. I just assumed he would want to come with me. I started auditioning for plays in Dallas and began to get roles, which encouraged me even more to make the move to Hollywood. So I just bided my time, working part-time as an English teacher at a language school and acting in plays.

The following fall, Adam convinced me to move to Austin and live with him during his final year of school. Honestly, it didn't take that much convincing, since I wanted to be with him no matter how or why or where. I had finally found my true love, and I was ready to build whatever future we envisioned together. It was like a dream.

Until four months later when we broke up.

SIX

SLOUCHING TOWARD HOLLYWOOD

My sin was this, that I looked for pleasure, beauty, and truth not in him but myself and his other creatures, and the search led me instead to pain, confusion, and error.
—AUGUSTINE, *CONFESSIONS*

[I resolved] to seek no knowledge other than that of which could be found in myself or else in the great book of the world, I spent the rest of my youth traveling . . . mixing with people of diverse temperaments and ranks, gathering various experiences, testing myself in the situations which fortune offered me, and at all times reflecting upon whatever came my way so as to derive some profit from it.
—RENÉ DESCARTES, *DISCOURSE ON THE METHOD*

BROKEN HEARTS CLUB

I thought moving in with Adam would be a dream come true, but instead, those were some of the most difficult months of my life. Things just weren't working out. I struggled to find a job in Austin, and living together brought out the worst in both of us. We fought much of the time about nothing in particular, and our love for each other slowly began to turn into contempt.

It was another cold day in December when we broke up. I moved back to Dallas the next day and was in a state of depression for several months. My heart was shattered, and I was inconsolable. It was the first time I had ever felt that distraught. I believed I was going to spend the rest of my life with Adam, and now it was over.

After about five months of this, I decided to forgo law school and move to Los Angeles. When I told my father that I was moving to pursue acting and writing, a look of pure puzzlement came over his face. He did not expect this, and he urged me to reconsider law school. But I told him my mind was made up. He didn't fight me on it and had an air of resignation about the whole thing. So I packed up my Volvo with all my possessions and headed to Hollywood.

GO WEST, YOUNG MAN

Ironically, Adam ended up driving out to Los Angeles with me. (My original plan!) He was going through a postcollege crisis and had copied my idea of moving to Tokyo to teach English while sorting out his life. By then our feelings for each other had dissipated (how fickle love is!), but we managed to remain friends. We drove together because he was leaving for Tokyo from Los Angeles.

After driving twenty-five hours straight, Adam and I finally arrived. It was a sunny late afternoon in June, and the air was crisp and cool. As we exited the I-10 freeway and drove up Fairfax Avenue, I felt utterly exhausted. But the exhilaration of being in this sprawling, storied city—my new city—far outweighed the fatigue of the long drive from Dallas. I was finally doing what I wanted to do, and pursuing what I wanted to pursue. I was about to embark on a new, wild adventure, and I was filled with anticipation and wonder. I had arrived, at least physically, if not figuratively.

One of my close friends from high school, Francesca, graciously let me stay at her place at Beverly and Fairfax (the Erewhon building!) until I got on my feet. The fact that she lived there largely influenced my decision to move. I don't know that I would have had the courage to do it without her encouragement and support. I crashed on a futon in her bedroom for a couple of months. Each night we would stay up late chatting about the day, about other friends, about the future. Francesca and I were close in high school, but in Los Angeles I became her GBF (gay best friend).

We were the real-life Will and Grace, always ready with a witty barb or a punch line, morning, noon, or night. We did everything together. We cheered each other on in our respective career paths, watched each other burn through way too many romantic relationships, and helped each other get through the day-to-day craziness of Hollywood. She unswervingly encouraged me to pursue my dreams and was always supportive of whatever boyfriend I had at the time, with all of whom she got along swimmingly.

Francesca helped me navigate this new world by getting me plugged into her friend group, which was made up mostly of artists, filmmakers, writers, and actors, all smart and talented, with a wry and razor-sharp sense of humor. These were my kind of folks. That was one of the hallmarks of my friendship with Francesca: we made each other laugh—a lot. She was one of the wittiest people I knew, not to mention one of the prettiest. She graduated from the most traditional and fancy all-girl prep school in Dallas, Hockaday, but her take on life and her interests were anything but traditional. She appreciated the absurd and the unconventional, maybe as a result of her being half Mexican and half white in an all-white school.

She would often tell the story of one classmate in high school whispering to another at the lunch table, "Isn't Francesca's mother Spanish?" This story would always get a big laugh from our friends because of how ridiculous the question was, and how it was whispered as if it were somehow scandalous that she could be ethnically diverse. But I think these kinds of remarks and attitudes had a bigger impact on

Francesca than maybe even she realized. I think that's why we bonded so deeply. I, too, despised the conventional because my unconventional sexuality prompted years and years of alienation. Growing up in Dallas, Francesca and I were both aliens in a land of homogeneity.

Los Angeles was the perfect antidote to Dallas. Diversity in thought, race, and sexual orientation was revered in this city. I felt a sense of complete freedom, both in my sexuality and in my creativity. It was a socially progressive, liberal town, and I didn't need to hide anything. If there was any lingering vestige of shame about my sexuality, Los Angeles rid me of it. I felt free to be me! Self-expression was highly regarded here, and a lot of people in Hollywood got paid very well for such expression, whether in writing, acting, directing, music, or other creative arts.

I was surrounded by like-minded people and felt the most like myself. I was finally home, and I began to flourish in that environment.

THE ARTIST'S WAY

Soon after my arrival, I enrolled in an acting class at Larry Moss Studio, run by one of the most renowned teachers in Hollywood. I enjoyed the challenge and the adrenaline rush that came from putting up scenes or monologues each week; it was terrifying and satisfying at the same time. I grew rapidly as a person in this creative crucible. My class was exactly what I had always imagined an acting class to be: a place of expression for a bunch of young, interesting, and slightly crazy artists who weren't afraid of exposing themselves and putting themselves out there. Each week the class would begin with acting exercises, such as lying on the ground meditating on some aspect of ourselves or a character, moving around the room as if we were a specific kind of animal, or singing whatever song popped into our heads. It was straight out of a movie! All these exploratory activities were extremely cathartic, leaving many students in tears.

Scene study exercises, in which students put up scenes and the class and the teacher would pick apart their performances, were even more intense, and the critiques were at times brutal. No one in class seemed to hold back when it came to ripping someone's performance to shreds, and their criticism of my performances left me in tears many times. But I loved it. I felt as if I was growing as a person. I began to see my strengths and weaknesses, not only in acting but in life in general. I was becoming more in touch with who I really was.

I soon discovered that one of my strengths was comedy, so I joined an improvisation class at the Groundlings, a legendary sketch comedy institution on Melrose Avenue. This took my fears to new heights. But, again, I loved the challenge and the excitement of walking a tightrope without a net. My experience at the Groundlings eventually kindled my love for writing.

FRIENDS

During this time, I supported myself by teaching English at a language school in Beverly Hills. It wasn't the most exciting job, but I didn't care; I had bigger things ahead. I found a beautiful apartment in a historical Spanish building in West Hollywood that had once been the home to luminaries such as James Dean and Marilyn Monroe. I felt it was the perfect place for a young aspiring actor!

I became very close friends with an extremely bright and witty guy named Jacob, whom I met through mutual friends. He, too, was gay and grew up in a conservative state. And like me, Los Angeles was a safe haven for him, a place to explore and be open about his sexuality. He let go of many inhibitions that he had pent up during his rigid upbringing, but I think he still felt he had let down his parents because of his sexual orientation. He didn't have an easy life during his formative years as I had. His parents were much more strict with him than my parents were with me, so he didn't have as much freedom. He also didn't have any confidants to share his secret with, leading him to simply repress his sexuality. When he moved to Los Angeles, he was still wrestling with a lot of shame regarding it. I was happy to see him slowly shed this shame as we thoroughly engaged in this permissive and unrestrained city. We rushed in where angels feared to tread.

I wanted everyone to be free to be who they were with wild abandon and without shame, completely comfortable in their own skin. And I was furious at those in society who tried to constrain or shame others for being who they were, not least of whom were on the religious right. They, I thought, were the reasons why many gays abuse alcohol and drugs, causing them to self-medicate the deeps wounds inflicted by their family's and society's rejection. I wanted to see an end to this kind of intolerance and oppression. I wanted nothing less than full liberation, full inclusion, and full acceptance in the mainstream.

Jacob and I became partners in crime in terms of gay life in Los Angeles. We frequented the plethora of gay bars and attended exclusive celebrity-laced Hollywood parties. We met interesting people and went to interesting places.

Another friend, Billy, loomed large in my life. If life were an orange, Billy not only sucked all the juice out of it but ate the rind as well—and wanted the tree it came from! He had a formidable presence and was extremely ambitious. I became close with his smart and fabulous group of friends from his alma mater, Brown University. He began his career as Diane Keaton's assistant and went on to become her producing partner. His wit was nonpareil, and his personality was larger than life. When we met at a party in the Hollywood Hills, we hit it off immediately and became great friends. He seemed to always be surrounded by a whirlwind of fun and drama. He was best friends with Minnie Driver at the height of her career, when she was nominated for an Oscar for her performance in *Good Will Hunting* with Matt Damon. For his birthday, about six of us, including Minnie, went to Cabo San Lucas to celebrate, where he had rented a big house near the beach. We had a blast hanging out at the house, frolicking on the beach, and dancing at the local nightclub (where paparazzi were stalking Minnie).

This was the life I always wanted, with glamorous friends and extraordinary experiences. I despised the banal, the mediocre, and the mundane. I wanted life at its best and most exciting. That's what we all wanted, and it was all happening. Screenplays were getting sold, movie roles were getting snagged, and films were getting produced. Most, if not all, of us went on to do extremely well in our respective fields. It was an exciting time for everyone.

None of us ever talked about God. Not once. It was understood that God probably didn't exist, and that Christianity was for people in flyover states. No, God was not on our radar, not even anywhere close. We were concerned about two things and two things only: success in our careers and success in our romances. Cool career and romantic love were our raisons d'être. Both were equally important and required a considerable amount of energy. At any given moment, most of us had one but not the other. It was rare to have both flourishing simultaneously, but when that did happen, life was great.

Even though I was also pretty ambitious, I focused more of my time and energy on relationships than career. I believed finding "the one," like what I thought I had with Adam, was what life was all about. I knew that someone out there would save me and give meaning to my life. I identified with Victor Frankl, who wrote about discovering the meaning of life in his acclaimed memoir, *Man's Search for Meaning*:

> . . . for the first time in my life I saw the truth as it is set into songs by so many poets, proclaimed as the final wisdom by so many thinkers. The truth—that love is the ultimate and the highest goal to which man can aspire. Then I grasped the greatest meaning of the greatest secret that human poetry and human thought and belief have to impart: *The salvation of man is through love and in love.* I understood how a man who has nothing left in this world still may know his bliss, be it only for a brief moment, in contemplation of his beloved.[1] (emphasis original)

I agreed with Frankl wholeheartedly. Since God was not an option for me, love from another human being was the only salve I could find for the longings of my soul. And so my mission in this world was to find that transcendent love and to know that bliss. The character Charles Ryder in *Brideshead*

Revisited put it another way: "To know and love one other human being is the root of all wisdom."[2] This was true in my relationship with Adam. I felt wiser because of it and understood the complexity of life in a deeper way. I knew I was onto something, so I kept searching.

BOYFRIENDS

Over the years in Los Angeles, I had a series of serious and intense relationships with four guys. But each relationship lasted roughly two years, and each had the same story arc. First six months of total bliss and second six months of slightly less bliss and slightly more reality. Toward the end of the first year, the relationship would begin to decline, the romantic period would be over, and the actual, real-life issues would emerge. After that, the relationship would devolve into fights, jealousy, and antipathy. And by the end of the second year, it would be over. It was the same over and over again.

What was interesting about this cycle was that with each new relationship, I had renewed hope. It was as if I had amnesia. Each time, I thought, *He is the one who will save me. He is the one who will bring meaning to my existence. He is the one who will last.* The playwright Sam Shepard came to the same conclusion while musing about his long relationship with actress Jessica Lange:

It's impossible the way people enter into it feeling they're going to be saved by the other one. And it seems like many, many times that quicksand happens in a relationship when you feel that somehow you can be saved.[3]

I was in that quicksand many times. I couldn't seem to figure the whole love thing out. I just kept on winding up back where I started, making the same mistakes, making the same bad choices, and, in the process, slowly losing my faith in humanity. But despite all this, I was still a hopeless romantic and an eternal optimist when it came to love—in other words, I was a masochist.

PRIDE

Every June from the late 1990s to the mid-2000s, my friends and I never missed the gay pride parades in Los Angeles, San Francisco, or New York, wherever we happened to be that year. Gay acceptance was on the rise and we wanted to be a part of it. As the years went by, the parades got bigger and better. I delighted in them because I felt I was part of something greater than myself, part of a critical movement. I remember being in New York one year for the parade and feeling a remarkable sense of giddiness and elation. I was in one of my favorite cities, participating in a significant cultural

phenomenon, connected to an important cause and cele-
bration. That day in particular, I really felt all the years of
alienation melt away as I watched the colorful characters pass
by. Sure, there were cheesy parts of the parade that I didn't
particularly like, but I was more interested in the political
repercussions of these global events. I was happy to be a part
of something that was changing the world's understanding of
who we were as individuals.

That same feeling of giddiness and elation struck me
another time when I was in New York. For a few years I spent
Christmas in New York with my best friend, Ryan, because
spending time with my family in Dallas made me slightly
depressed; I simply felt I didn't belong. So going to New York
was a great antidote to the traditional Christmas with the
family. The bitter cold winters in New York didn't bother me
a bit, and I was excited to be there. One year, on Christmas
Eve, Ryan and I went out to dinner and then to various gay
bars downtown. We were both night owls by nature, so staying out late, especially while on vacation, was de rigueur. We
ended the night at a gay bar in the East Village, staying there
until six in the morning. The owner gave each of us a glass
of champagne on the house to ring in Christmas morning. I
remember feeling truly happy at that moment, being as far
from a conventional Christmas morning as one could get.
We sipped the champagne and let the buzz carry us into
Christmas Day.

A FEW HIGHLIGHTS

Living in Los Angeles was the roller coaster ride of a lifetime. I had so many wonderful experiences and met so many amazing people. I attended movie premieres as a regular part of my social calendar. I saw friends, met celebrities, and sipped cocktails, not to mention enjoying amazing free food. I attended the Grammys and went to the Golden Globe afterparties and to the Governor's Ball after the Oscars. I rode with Nia Vardalos in her limo from the Oscars to the legendary Vanity Fair Oscar party the year she was nominated for her role in *My Big Fat Greek Wedding*. I spent summers swimming in Drew Barrymore's pool in the Hollywood Hills.

I was invited to a party Prince threw at his house in Benedict Canyon, where he performed for several hours on a stage set up in his enormous backyard; a small affair with remarkably few guests, considering. I vacationed at Diane Keaton's desert getaway home. For many summers, Mariska Hargitay would let me stay at her place in New York while she was on hiatus from her television show, *Law & Order: SVU*. I attended Paris Hilton's small engagement party when she was engaged to the Greek shipping heir Paris Latsis.

I acted opposite Nick Offerman, from *Parks and Recreation*, in a movie that premiered at the Sundance Film Festival. I attended a cocktail party at the home of Arianna Huffington of the *Huffington Post*, who greeted each and every person as they walked through the front door. I remember telling her she was my favorite person in Los Angeles. She responded with a smile, and a "Thank you, dahling." I felt welcome in her grand Brentwood estate filled with the liberal elite of Los Angeles, all of whom shared the same progressive politics, wanted to change the world, and demanded more freedom, especially concerning gay rights.

One summer, while I was vacationing in Paris, an old American friend who had long been an expat there invited me to a Bastille Day party at the home of the renowned and hugely respected fashion designer Rick Owens. He and his wife, Michèle Lamy (who was also his muse), lived in a beautiful five-story mansion on the Place du Palais Bourbon in central Paris. When I entered the foyer, the first thing I noticed was a life-size, anatomically correct, nude wax sculpture of Rick himself! I spent the day chatting with Rick and Michèle and their interesting guests, while sipping wine and dining on the Moroccan feast Michèle had delivered. Michèle's daughter, Scarlett Rouge, took me on a tour of Rick's design studio on the upper floors of their château, and I was awestruck by his incredible work. Experiences like these were not only fun and exciting, but they also gave me a sense of meaning and importance.

After years of struggling to make it as an actor/writer in Hollywood, I eventually fell into a career as a set designer through a friend who was the West Coast fashion editor at the *New York Times Magazine*. I began by helping out on her shoots with anything that needed to be done: packing boxes, steaming clothes, lugging clothing racks, and so on. She then started to give me more responsibilities, including finding props for fashion shoots. I was surprised when she told me that I had a really good eye, and that everything I picked out was exactly what she had in mind, which made me think I might be good at this. I soon began building simple sets, which were received well, followed by sets that were more artistically complicated and logistically involved. I was delighted that my work was receiving positive responses from photographers, clients, and talent. Soon after, my newfound career took off, and the jobs and the money began to pour in. It was nice to happen upon a vocation that I not only enjoyed, but for which I was also well compensated. I finally hit my stride and began to flourish.

As a set designer, I worked with many stars, including Meryl Streep, Katy Perry, Carrie Underwood, Christina Aguilera, Nicole Richie, Paris Hilton, Nicole Kidman, Kate Beckinsale, Jessica Chastain, Natalie Portman, and Oprah Winfrey; and for many fashion magazines, such as *Vogue* and *Harper's Bazaar*. I also worked with many supermodels, such as Claudia Schiffer, Guinevere Van Seenus, and Cindy Crawford. My job took me to many interesting places around the world. I once worked on a three-month photo shoot divided into two-week stints in Chicago, New York, Bangkok, Manila, Hong Kong, and Beijing, where we spent one day photographing an opulent dinner party on the Great Wall of China!

All these extraordinary experiences were great fun and sustained me for a long time. I was having a ball. What more could I have asked out of life? If I had been given the option of planning my life and career when I was younger, I never could have dreamed of such opportunities and experiences that had become my daily life!

But lurking underneath all this, deep in the recesses of my mind and heart, was a longing that had yet to be satisfied.

SEVEN

IS THAT ALL THERE IS?

Things fall apart; the centre cannot hold.
—WILLIAM BUTLER YEATS,
"THE SECOND COMING"

Over the course of a three-month photo shoot that took me all over the world, I became very close with the photographer's assistant, Jake, a young English bloke. He and I hit it off immediately. Being from London, he had a naturally deft sense of humor, which I thoroughly appreciated, and I was the first gay guy he had ever befriended. We spent a lot of time together; if we weren't working, we would take off and explore whatever city we were in. Bangkok proved to be the most fun. We discovered an exclusive nightclub that became our nightly destination for drinking and dancing. Jake began to shed any homophobia that lingered from his childhood in England and enjoyed our friendship immensely. He peppered me with questions about my sexual orientation, and I did my best to help him understand. By the end of the trip, he had fully embraced gay culture.

I felt like I had helped him out of the Dark Ages into an enlightened understanding of homosexuality, a lifestyle I was living and enjoying thoroughly—or at least I thought I was. Despite many wonderful and exciting experiences, I still felt like something was missing. I had no explanation for it. I couldn't have dreamed of asking for more, yet everything somehow felt hazy. Though I didn't articulate them, the questions kept coming. *Who am I? What am I doing here? What's the meaning of life?*

I needed answers to these questions, so I spent many years and lots of money trying to find them.

PSYCHOTHERAPY: SEEKING ANSWERS FROM WITHIN

The unexamined life is not worth living.

—Plato, *Apology*

One of the ways I endeavored to shed light on the murkiness of life was through psychotherapy. After several failed relationships and a general vexation about life's meaning, I decided to seek professional help. I was sure someone with a PhD would have some answers. I also wanted to get to know myself, because I thought maybe that's why I was here: to know myself as completely as possible, to understand what makes me tick, and to get at the root of my various and sundry issues. Maybe life was all about this journey of self-discovery.

A trusted friend referred me to a therapist, whose office was conveniently close, less than a mile from my apartment, and who happened to be gay. One day a week for five years, I spent fifty minutes ruminating, complaining, and crying about my childhood, my relationships, and my career. And each week he would help me as best he could to process the vast and complex terrain of my psyche. For the first few years, I found the time profitable. He helped me uncover possible motivations for certain behaviors that seemed to be a pattern in my life, such as why I chose to date the same wounded-bird type of guy *every* time. What drew me to that? Why did all my romantic relationships live in this sliver of neurotic space? Why were these relationships so tortured? He helped me connect the dots to many of these questions.

The dots invariably found their way back to my mother, the definition of a wounded bird. We had a boundaryless, codependent relationship. Because my father was aloof much of the time, my mother turned to me, her youngest son, to fill the void he left behind. And what son doesn't want his mother to need him? In many ways, I was her surrogate husband. Of course, this dynamic did not portend well for my emotional health as an adult.

These kinds of things seemed to help me understand my decision-making processes more and more. But as the years went on, I began to realize that knowing myself, however helpful, was not the answer, or at least, not the ultimate answer. I was getting answers to the *how*, but the *what* and *why* of life still eluded me. Even though I was discovering interesting idiosyncrasies about myself, I was still just going in circles, never truly reaching an end, never formulating a cohesive theory that could explain the meaning of life—the meaning of *my* life! I felt I was just rehashing the same things over and over. But to what end? What was the point of this therapy? Was it all simply an exercise in futility, costing me a fortune? There's only so many years one can talk about one's mother! I began to want real answers, answers that were outside of myself: Why am I *actually* here? Where am I *actually* going?

My therapist never had any answers, just questions. I remember being extremely frustrated in his office one day, and I came right out and screeched, "What am I doing here? What is this all for? What's the meaning of life?"

He paused, then responded in his typical, irritating and unhelpful way, "What do *you* think the meaning of life is?"

I finally snapped. I said, "I quit! I'm done," then walked out of his office and never went back.

THEATER OF THE ABSURD: SEEKING ANSWERS FROM WITHOUT

I enjoyed fables and fictions, which could only graze the skin.

—AUGUSTINE, *CONFESSIONS*

Another place I turned to in my quest for answers was the theater. I often traveled to New York and sometimes London and took in as many plays as I could when there. Serious plays by serious playwrights, such as Pinter, Stoppard, Albee, O'Neill, Ibsen, and so on. I thought these brilliant guys would help me get to some sort of truth through their intelligent and complex work. Every time I watched a play, I felt close to grasping some eternal truth. But invariably, just as I was feeling it was within reach, it would fall apart. The truth somehow could never fully hold together. It lacked coherence, at least in an ultimate sense—that is, in explaining the true meaning of life. These plays would often address ultimate questions, but in the end, could never really answer them.

I attended part 1 of Tony Kushner's epic play *Angels in America* in London's West End, and part 2 on Broadway in New York. I, of course, was deeply moved by this politically charged, gay-themed drama. But even after the six hours of dizzying dialogue, I found it wanting.

This frustrating phenomenon kept happening over and over. I would arrive at the theater with a sense of optimism and hope but would leave feeling frustrated and despondent; never really getting the answers I wanted, and often leaving with more questions. A nice dinner afterward always proved to be a good antidote to the frustration (with a glass of wine or two).

Art had a similar effect on me. Whenever I was in New York, London, or Paris, I would make the Museum of Modern Art, Tate Modern, or Centre Pompidou one of my first visits. I loved the modernists, but it was the conceptual artists, such as Marcel Duchamp, Jeff Koons, Cindy Sherman, John Baldessari, and Yayoi Kusama, who really got me excited. I remember going to MoMA in New York and having my breath taken away by a few small paintings by a relatively new artist named John Currin; I actually wept while staring at his satirical figurative paintings. While at the Centre Pompidou in Paris, I happened upon a Yves Klein exhibition, which consisted of several empty galleries with their walls painted white; I almost passed out from the sheer genius of it.

Art often moved me like this. I would be elevated a hair's breadth above the ground while experiencing these extraordinary works. I would feel some sort of connection to the spiritual; indeed, art was a spiritual experience for me. Museums and theaters were my temples of choice, my places of worship. And even though that worship was at times transcendent and sublime, it never quite reached the face of God, as it were.

I'm reminded of C. S. Lewis's words:

> We want something else which can hardly be put into words—to be united with the beauty we see, to pass into it, to receive it into ourselves, to bathe in it, to become part of it. . . . That is why the poets tell us such lovely falsehoods. They talk as if the west wind could really sweep into the human soul; but it can't.[1]

PARIS: THE DENOUEMENT

All my searching was leading me back to the same place: nowhere. And time was no longer on my side. The older I got, the less and less these kinds of explorations and experiences satisfied me. The law of diminishing returns was starting to set in.

Nothing made this more apparent than when I was in Paris for fashion week in March 2009. I attended several runway shows and plenty of after-parties. One night, an epiphany struck me during Stella McCartney's soiree at a club in Saint-Germain-des-Prés. The place was packed. I was sipping champagne at a small table with Rachel Zoe, the famed Hollywood fashion stylist and reality TV star, and her husband, Rodger. Our table was perched a few steps above the dance floor populated with the who's who of the fashion world, all gyrating to the throbbing music.

After socializing for a couple of hours, I took a moment to look around and contemplate the scene. In this sea of beautiful people, I suddenly felt an intense sense of emptiness. I'm not exactly sure what brought it on, but there I was, in the middle of Paris at an ultrachic fashion party, feeling dead inside.

For a moment, utter panic filled my body. I thought, *If this stuff isn't doing it for me anymore, what on earth will? I've done everything, met everyone, been everywhere. What am I going to do for the next fifty or sixty years of my life?* I was running out of options. I felt numb and had to get out of the place. I got up from the table without saying goodbye to Rachel or Rodger and ghosted. I hopped in a taxi and headed back to the apartment I had rented in the Marais. Later I sat up in bed, unable to sleep, wishing I smoked cigarettes because it would have been a great time for that.

I stayed up all night pondering the future, and the future seemed bleak. Tolstoy's words in *A Confession* rang true to me: "One can only live while one is intoxicated with life; as soon as one is sober it is impossible not to see that it is all a mere fraud and a stupid fraud!"[2]

A few days later I returned to Los Angeles, and slowly eased back into my routine. The busyness of life with work and friends drowned out any existential angst. A general unease about the future still lingered, but for the most part, I was able to keep those thoughts at bay.

Little did I know that six months later, a random meeting at a coffee shop in Silver Lake would lead to all the answers I was seeking. My existential angst would finally be addressed. For good.

EIGHT

FALLOUT

*I believe in Christianity as I believe that the
Sun has risen, not only because I see it but
because by it I see everything else.*
—C. S. Lewis, *The Weight of Glory*

When God saved me on that day in 2009, I was in a state
of euphoria. I felt like I was floating on a cloud. It was as if
my whole life had been in black and white but now everything was suddenly in color. The haze had finally lifted and I
could see the horizon. I was filled with hope and excitement.
But now I had the daunting task of informing all my dear,
liberal, progressive, atheist friends that I was a born-again
Christian. I was sure none of them would ever want to speak
to me again.

   Over the following month, I met one-on-one with each
of them and shared this completely unexpected and joyous

news. When I told them I had some major, life-changing news, they responded with questions like, "Are you moving?" "Are you buying a house?" "Did you meet someone?" I told them, yes, I had moved, to the kingdom of light from the kingdom of darkness. Yes, I had a new house, the "house of the LORD" (Ps. 23:6), where I shall dwell forever. Yes, I had in fact met someone, Jesus Christ. None of them, not in their wildest imaginations, expected such answers. Not one. My old friend Jacob brusquely responded, "I'm happy for you, but don't *ever* try to proselytize me." Francesca's first question to me after I told her I had met the God of the universe was, "You're not pro-life now, are you?"

All of them were shocked, but for the most part they were lovely about it and genuinely happy for me. With a couple of exceptions, they didn't want to embark on their own search for the truth, but much to my surprise, they still wanted to remain friends. I'm still close to many of them to this day.

Lisa, my friend from Dallas who came to live with me in Tokyo, messaged me on Facebook when she heard the news: "Word on the street is that lots is going on with you. . . . Tell me about you." I wrote her back, detailing the entire account of my conversion, and sent her several sermons to listen to. Later we spoke on the phone, and she told me she "wanted what I had." I was thrilled by her desire to know God and spent time explaining the gospel to her, answering her questions, and praying with her. By the grace of God, she is now a Christian!

I could not control myself from sharing the gospel while working on photo shoots. I told everyone on the set about Jesus and shared my testimony with anyone and everyone who would listen. I had the best news in the world to share, and I was going to share it! I no longer saw work as just a means to make money but as an opportunity to share the good news. Several people I worked with on shoots came to know Christ; others are still seeking, slowly.

Immediately after my encounter with Jesus, I worked on a two-week shoot, during which I told my assistant, Simon, the whole story. I exclaimed, "Simon! God is real! Jesus is real!"

But he wasn't convinced. I spent the next ten days talking with him about Jesus and eagerly invited him to church. He politely declined. Then, six months later, I got a surprising text from him saying he and his wife wanted to come to my church's Easter service! I was stunned, and very excited. They both showed up that Easter, and his wife, Sally, ended up coming to Christ. Although Simon earnestly continued attending church every Sunday for the next couple of years, as far as I know, he hasn't given his life to Christ. We are still praying for him.

While working on another photo shoot in summer 2010, I had a lengthy conversation with a makeup artist, Annie, with whom I had worked on a couple of shoots earlier that year. As we chatted throughout the day between shots, she asked if I was doing any traveling over the summer. I told her

I was going on a prayer tour in London with my church, where we would walk around in small groups and pray for the city, and then, in the evening, come back together for a sermon and worship. She was taken aback when I mentioned this, but she was downright shocked when I shared my testimony. She asked, "But what about being gay? Why would you be a part of something that was against who you were?" She found it remarkable, even bizarre, that a gay man would leave that life to follow Christ. When I told her how by finding Jesus I finally found the love and fulfillment I had been looking for, it shook her up. Her closest friends over the years in New York and Los Angeles were perfectly happy being gay, and she couldn't understand what compelled me to believe such a thing. Honestly, her reaction to all of it was exactly the same as mine had been.

A few days after the shoot, I left for London. Before I left, though, I emailed Annie a few sermons that I thought would be beneficial for her to hear. When I returned, we met for coffee. She was clearly intrigued but understandably had many questions. Could there really be a God? How do you know? She was at a point in her life where she had more or less reached her professional goals and accomplished pretty much everything she set out to do. Yet she had that same nagging question: Is that all there is?

I invited her to church, but she was busy and reluctant. A couple of months and a ten-day shoot later, however, she came to church with me. She said she had a good experience and found the sermon relatable, but I could tell she was still hesitant. Nevertheless, she kept coming back to church every Sunday. On December 1, 2010, I texted her an invitation to the weekly Bible study I attended in Silver Lake, which she accepted. I picked her up, and we headed over to the group. I kept an eye on her during the study that night, and I could tell a storm was a-brewin' in her heart.

When we got back into my car, she announced, "I've made a commitment tonight."

I was excited, obviously, but I wanted to be sure what she meant, so asked, "To this Bible study group?"

"No, to Jesus!"

Whoa!

That very night, she had moved from darkness into light. Born again. Saved. Everything about Christianity made sense to her. She seemed like a totally different person; even her countenance seemed to have brightened. After that night, she was consumed with a desire to know more about God. She devoured her Bible and listened to sermons round the clock. Her whole life changed—not to mention her eternity!

To this day, I'm still in shock that God came into my life. I think of that September day every time I see one of my friends encounter Jesus. I'm in constant awe that he showed grace to me and saved me, and I wake up every morning with a deep sense of gratitude. I still have ups and downs in my life, but underneath it all is an indestructible joy.

THE CALLING

At the end of 2013, I began to feel God calling me to go to seminary. At first I just ignored it, because back in January 2012, kind of on a whim, I started a men's clothing line called Doodles Homme, with JT, a friend from my community group (Bible study). Neither of us had ever designed a clothing line, so it was a steep learning curve. But Doodles Homme took off surprisingly fast, and we quickly got into high-end, exclusive stores in Los Angeles and New York, as well as the legendary boutique, Colette, in Paris. With its success, we were well on our way to becoming a worldwide brand, which made me resistant to seminary. The call, however, was getting stronger and stronger. It was as if I were on a train headed to seminary and couldn't get off.

At the beginning of 2014, I approached Nick, one of the elders at my church, and explained the situation. I told him, "I feel like God is calling me to seminary, but I'm not sure what to do. Doodles Homme is doing well, and I would have to shut down the brand if I do this because of the demanding time commitment. Also, how will it all work financially? I'd have to turn down most of my production design jobs because of school." He immediately prayed for me. Afterward, he told me he sensed that God was going to pay for me to attend seminary, and that it would be the confirmation I was supposed to go. I thought, *What? How could that be? How is God going to pay for seminary?* Clearly, Nick was off his rocker.

Nevertheless, I soon called JT and told him I was going to enroll in seminary and so had to quit Doodles Homme. I asked him if he wanted to take over the company, but he said he had been moving toward creating his own brand that was a huge departure from Doodles Homme designwise, and so we decided to dissolve the company. I was sad but also really excited about this new adventure God was taking me on.

I applied to Talbot School of Theology at Biola University and received an acceptance letter a few months later. Just as Nick predicted, from my enrollment in fall 2014 to my graduation in December 2017, I never paid a penny for school. God had used his people to rally around me and contribute to my seminary fund. It was an amazing testament to the idea that if you step out in faith and are obedient to God's call, he will provide. The whole experience was not only extremely humbling, but it also greatly encouraged my faith. The solid theological and biblical training I received at Talbot guides me when I speak at churches and universities on the subject of homosexuality, especially when answering difficult questions on this complex subject. I continue to do production design jobs to pay the rent, but itinerant speaking and teaching is my passion and vocation.

I can't explain all the ways my life has changed, but I want to try to give you a sense of what God has done in my life since my conversion. A person simply does not have an encounter with Jesus and remain the same. The changes I've experienced happened in ways you might expect, and others you might not.

PART TWO

REFLECTIONS

See to it that no one takes you captive by philosophy
and empty deceit, according to human tradition,
according to the elemental spirits of the world, and
not according to Christ.

—COLOSSIANS 2:8

Since becoming a Christian, I've spent a good bit of time pondering the complexity of the challenging issue of homosexuality. Certain biblical passages have leaped out at me, passages that don't address homosexuality directly but have impacted my understanding of it.

My goal is to explore every possible angle and uncover blind spots for believers and skeptics alike. With the assault of media and culture that surrounds and inundates us, we can lose sight of not only biblical truths, but also inconsistencies in our own worldviews. It is my hope that the chapters that follow will aid you in gaining a more fully orbed understanding of one of the most important subjects of our time.

In the last chapter, I offer my thoughts on how Christians can respond to those who struggle with homosexuality, to friends and family members who come out, and to the LGBT community at large; each group requires a slightly different approach. I have been a member of all of them at various points in my life. I know what it's like to struggle with same-sex attraction. I know what it's like to come out to Christian parents. And I know what it's like to feel marginalized by Christians while within the LGBT community. But I also know what it's like to have victory in Christ.

Because I've lived the life of a man who once fully

identified as gay, and now, because of the power of the gospel, live as a new creation in Christ, I feel equipped to help educate others on how to handle these tough situations we encounter as Christians in the twenty-first century. My identity is no longer in my sexuality but in Christ, and I choose to live in a manner that is biblical and glorifying to him. My hope is that, after reading this book, you will be better equipped to navigate the tension between truth and love in a healthy, balanced way.

NINE

JUST THE FAQs

Since my conversion to Christ, I have been asked many questions about my relationship with Jesus in regard to my sexuality. This is usually the first place an inquisitor goes when he or she discovers that I'm a Christian. Much to my chagrin, I rarely hear the questions that I find more interesting, like, "Why did God become a human being?" or "What's it like to know the Creator of the universe?" No, the first question is usually something along the lines of, "But you're still gay, right?" or "You can still date guys, right?" Now, I'm not diminishing the curiosity that prompts such a question (indeed, I asked the very same question), especially given the culture we're in, but it would be nice to be asked once in a while about the ample evidence for the resurrection of Jesus or the indisputable reliability of the New Testament documents!

In this chapter, I will endeavor to answer some of the

most common questions I hear from believers and non-believers alike.

ISN'T IT UNFAIR THAT YOU HAVE TO BE ALONE FOR THE REST OF YOUR LIFE?

First, I'm not alone. I am in a personal relationship with the King of the universe—the best and most exciting relationship I've ever been in! A relationship that makes all human relationships pale in comparison. A relationship that is transcendent, fulfilling, and completely satisfying: "Whoever drinks of the water that I will give him will never be thirsty again" (John 4:14). He never cheats on me, he's always faithful, and he will never leave or forsake me! (All that cannot be said about my ex-boyfriends.) In fact, we are so close that he dwells in my heart: "Do you not realize this about yourselves, that Jesus Christ is in you?" (2 Cor. 13:5). I wholeheartedly echo Paul's words:

> I count everything as loss because of the surpassing worth of knowing Christ Jesus my Lord. For his sake I have suffered the loss of all things and count them as rubbish, in order that I may gain Christ. (Phil. 3:8)

To put it plainly, feeling entitled to a nice house, a great job, and a fabulous romantic partner is a particularly American phenomenon. It's what we're told daily by television, movies, billboards, and magazines. "I deserve this, I deserve that," is the common refrain. I have come to realize, as the Bible describes, that I deserve nothing, and yet in my brokenness Jesus came to give me everything. So being "alone" for the rest of my life is not unfair. What's unfair is that Jesus had to be beaten and crucified for my sins. What's unfair is that God had mercy on me, a wicked rebel. What's unfair is that I get to have an intimate relationship with Jesus. What's unfair is that on the last day, when he returns to judge the world, I will be declared innocent before a holy God because of Christ's righteousness.

It's easy to forget that Jesus was single, poor, and homeless. The apostle Paul also was single, and his life was no cakewalk either:

> Five times I received at the hands of the Jews the forty lashes less one. Three times I was beaten with rods. Once I was stoned. Three times I was shipwrecked; a night and a day I was adrift at sea; on frequent journeys, in danger from rivers, danger from robbers, danger from my own people, danger from Gentiles, danger in the city, danger in the wilderness, danger at sea, danger from false brothers; in toil and hardship, through many a sleepless night, in hunger and thirst, often without food, in cold and exposure. (2 Cor. 11:24–27)

I seriously doubt Paul thought his life was unfair. In his letter to the Romans, he said, "I consider that the sufferings of this present time are not worth comparing with the glory that is to be revealed to us" (Rom. 8:18). He continued in his second letter to the Corinthians: "This light momentary affliction is preparing for us an eternal weight of glory beyond all comparison" (2 Cor. 4:17).

Paul understood what he had to look forward to and was happy to be a servant of Christ Jesus. He didn't spend his days wallowing in self-pity. He focused on spreading the gospel and planting churches. His sole desire was to advance the kingdom of God. So, do I think my life is unfair? Quite the contrary. I feel like the luckiest guy in the world!

Then there's this: I'm not alone, because I'm part of a family of fellow believers. I'm part of the body of Christ. When I was saved, I became a member of this new spiritual family, in which we encourage one another and bear each other's burdens. Whenever I'm struggling with anything, I simply reach out to one of my brothers or sisters in Christ and ask for help and prayer. I feel buoyed by the amazing group of Christians God has put in my life. I am incredibly blessed to have such an amazing body of believers at my church. I often get texts that simply say, "Praying for you today" or other encouraging words. This community helps sustain me while I'm on this journey to the celestial city.

Paul summed it up well in his letter to the Ephesian church:

> You are no longer strangers and aliens, but you are fellow citizens with the saints and members of the household of

God, built on the foundation of the apostles and prophets, Christ Jesus himself being the cornerstone, in whom the whole structure, being joined together, grows into a holy temple in the Lord. In him you also are being built together into a dwelling place for God by the Spirit. (Eph. 2:19–22)

Have I left behind a certain type of relationships? Absolutely. But have I cut myself off from meaningful relationships? Not even close! Jesus promises that every relationship I release for his sake will be given back to me a hundredfold in the church (Mark 10:29–30). The church can be a messy place, but I have been adopted into a family, and I would be a fool to reject that to cling to something I used to long for.

BUT AREN'T YOU BORN GAY?

This is a tricky one. I have vacillated among three different views throughout my life. Is there a gay gene? Is it due to environmental factors? Is it hormonal? When I was much younger, I thought I was gay because of environmental reasons: an unhealthy attachment to my mother, a distant relationship with my father, homosexual friends, and so on. As I got older, I was convinced I was born gay. I remember having a conversation with my father about it in my thirties, as I was planning to bring a boyfriend home for Christmas one year. This sparked an emergency meeting among some of my family members, in which a few of my siblings voiced their absolute opposition to the idea of my boyfriend attending our family Christmas. When my mother informed me about the controversy, I demanded she put my father on the phone. After I threatened to boycott Christmas with my family altogether, my father assured me that everything would be okay. During that conversation, I declared with absolute confidence, "Dad, you know I was born this way, right?"

But was I right? The simple answer is, nobody knows. No scientist worth his or her salt would claim any one of these reasons—biological, hormonal, or environmental—as *the* factor or even the prevailing factor for homosexuality. The renowned, openly gay scientist Dr. Richard Pillard, who has something to gain from a genetic link to homosexuality, conceded in a recent interview, "It's really hard to come up with any definite statement about [homosexuality]. I think some sort of genetic influence seems very likely, but beyond that, what really can we say? And the answer is: not a lot."[1]

Even Wikipedia, the most accessible source of general information, states the following:

The relationship between biology and sexual orientation is a subject of research. *A simple and singular determinant for sexual orientation has not been conclusively demonstrated*; various studies point to different, even conflicting positions, but scientists hypothesize that a combination of genetic, hormonal, and social factors determine sexual orientation.[2] (emphasis mine)

So the only thing that's clear is that it is unclear. No matter how many times Lady Gaga sings her gay anthem, "Born This Way," it still doesn't make it true. It's just plain sloppy to make claims like this. Of course, we don't expect pop stars to be scientifically or philosophically consistent, but the incessant refrain that one is born gay has a vast impact on culture.

What if someday a distinguished scientist discovers a gay gene? Then what? My response would be, "So what?" A finding like this would in no way affect my conviction that homosexual behavior is sinful. The Bible teaches that when human beings rebelled against God, this sin corrupted not only mankind but all of creation. Because of this, we all enter the world with broken appetites and disoriented urges. "Behold, I was brought forth in iniquity, and in sin did my mother conceive me" (Ps. 51:5); this is known as the doctrine of original sin. The Bible also teaches that every part of us—body, mind, will, and spirit—is corrupted by sin; this is known as the doctrine of total depravity. We are all fallen to the core, even our genes. One need only look at genetic birth defects to see one of the results of this radical corruption. Therefore it is moot whether or not a person is born gay. The "is" does not imply "ought." We're all born in sin.

One very important thing I must point out, however, is

that homosexual desire or orientation is *not* a choice. I never consciously chose to be attracted to men. In fact, my life would have been a lot easier had I not been. At first, I tried *not* to be gay. But due to the variety of factors I have already explained, my sexual desires were directed toward men. My decision to *act* on this desire was, of course, a choice, but without being indwelt by the Holy Spirit, that choice seemed uncontrollable. In other words, it felt completely natural for me to pursue sexual relations with men. As the American poet Emily Dickinson put it, "The heart wants what it wants."[3]

But upon my conversion, God gave me a new heart and put his Spirit in me (Ezek. 36:26), and that transformed what my heart wanted. Now my heart wants to be obedient to God, not conform to the passions of my former ignorance; in other words, to be holy because God is holy (1 Peter 1:14–16). My heart wants to please him because of the great love with which he loved me (Eph. 2:4). My heart wants to present my body as a living sacrifice, holy and acceptable to him (Rom. 12:1).

DIDN'T GOD CREATE YOU THAT WAY?

Since I'm asked this specific question often, I will address it as precisely as I can. God created us in his image—"God created man in his own image, in the image of God he created him" (Gen. 1:27)—but he surely did not create me gay.

As I mentioned, the fall had a deeply corrupting effect on humankind and marred that image. The corruption of my sexuality, along with every other aspect of my being, is a result of that fall. My sexuality is corrupted and broken in the most fundamental sense because of original sin. I am certain that homosexual desire is not what God intended for my life. It's just one of many symptoms of the fall. And just as God did not create me gay, he also, for example, did not create heterosexuals with the desire to objectify women as sexual objects for selfish pleasure. We see this exemplified throughout society with rampant addiction to pornography. Neither is right simply because it exists. It is a gross misunderstanding to believe that anything that *feels* natural is righteous.

Death wasn't in God's original plan either, but the fall brought death into the world too. "Just as sin came into the world through one man, and death through sin, and so death spread to all men because all sinned" (Rom. 5:12). The same goes for sickness and suffering. But this "de-creation" will all be rectified on the last day, when God creates the new heaven and the new earth. On that day, all brokenness will be fixed: "He will wipe away every tear from their eyes, and death shall be no more, neither shall there be mourning, nor crying, nor pain anymore, for the former things have passed away" (Rev. 21:4).

DOESN'T GOD WANT
YOU TO BE HAPPY?

According to the world, happiness is based on circumstances, which makes it temporal and fleeting. If our circumstances are good, then we are happy; if they are bad, then we are unhappy. When I was in relationships with men, my happiness fluctuated wildly based on how the relationship was going, which kept me strapped into the seat of an emotional roller coaster.

The Bible, however, speaks of a joy that is permanent, not based on circumstances but on the immutability of God as our Father, Jesus as our Savior, and the Holy Spirit as our Comforter. "Though you do not now see him, you believe in him and rejoice with joy that is inexpressible and filled with glory" (1 Peter 1:8). I always tell people that no matter how difficult things get for me or how stressed out I am, I have a permanent layer of joy in my gut that is impenetrable and indestructible. Jesus is my Rock.

That said, Jesus doesn't promise us happiness. He instead speaks frequently of the difficulty we will face if we are to be his disciples. "If anyone would come after me, let him deny himself and *take up his cross* and follow me" (Matt. 16:24, emphasis mine). In John 16:33, Jesus said, "In the world you will have tribulation." Peter also warned us, "Do not be surprised at the fiery trial when it comes upon you to test you, as though something strange were happening to you" (1 Peter 4:12).

What's more, our Father in heaven cares for us and guides us toward what's best for our lives, just as a good earthly father does for his child. A toddler might want to run all over the place, including into the street, but his father knows that it's dangerous, even deadly, to do so; therefore, he places limits on his child, whom he loves deeply. In the same way, God sets up limits for his children because he loves us and knows that we need them. If we go outside those boundaries, we risk pain, suffering, and death. For example, God instituted the covenant of marriage between one man and one woman. So if the husband goes outside of that covenantal boundary and has an affair with another woman, all kinds of pain and destruction will follow: the wife will be traumatized, which often leads to divorce; the kids' lives will be torn apart; and the emotional health of everyone involved will be jeopardized. This is what happens when we go outside of God's will.

God created sex to be enjoyed within the context of that covenantal marriage between a man and a woman. He doesn't restrict sex to this model just to be some kind of cosmic killjoy. He does it because he knows that within that covenant, a man and a woman can be naked physically, emotionally, and spiritually without fear of rejection. I don't think we realize as a culture how damaging it is emotionally, not to mention physically (for example, STDs), to engage in casual sex. We may think it's no big deal, but it leads to a lot of unnecessary pain and suffering for both parties involved.

In our contemporary culture, the operating notion in

marriage, or in any romantic relationship for that matter, is quid pro quo. As long as I have great biceps and you have great abs, then we're good. But if you lose those abs, I'm out! This example may seem absurd, but the underlying logic is quite real: as long as I'm getting what I want out of this marriage, all is well, but as soon as this is not the case, it's over. Time and time again, we find that God knew what was best after all. He created the universe and he created us. So he probably knows what he is doing.

Finally, just as a child derives joy from being obedient to his father, Christians, too, derive joy from being obedient to God. I actually find it joyful to obey him. "I delight to do your will, O my God; your law is within my heart" (Ps. 40:8). I feel safe within his boundaries. Just as a father has his child's best interests at heart, so our heavenly Father has his children's best interests at heart. I trust him with everything, including my life. He is my joy. Happiness is flimsy, but the joy of the Lord is rock solid. The journey to the celestial city may not be easy, but it's absolutely worth it.

BUT AREN'T WE SUPPOSED TO FOLLOW OUR HEARTS AND BE TRUE TO OURSELVES?

I was at a restaurant in Hollywood recently, one that I frequent quite a bit, and the hostess was wearing a sweater with the phrase "Follow your heart" knit across the front. I asked my waiter, with whom I had a friendly rapport, to look over at the hostess and read what was embroidered on her sweater. He did. Then I asked him if he thought the advice was good, bad, or neutral.

He considered it for a moment and said, "I would say neutral to good."

I challenged him. I told him that Hitler followed his heart when he ordered the execution of six million Jews; Stalin followed his heart when he oversaw the execution of nearly 700,000 people during the Great Purge in the former Soviet Union; Tiger Woods followed his heart when he had multiple extramarital affairs; and Bill Clinton followed his heart when he had "sexual relations with that woman, Miss Lewinsky" in the Oval Office.

He made a facial expression that communicated, "You have a point."

The problem with following our hearts is that, according to the Bible (and realistically), our hearts are "deceitful above all things, and desperately sick" (Jer. 17:9). Because of sin, our hearts are corrupt. This doesn't mean that everyone is as bad as they can possibly be at every possible moment. But as a rule, following our hearts—without the constraint and guidance of the Holy Spirit—is at best unreliable and at worst dangerous. This is what the apostle Paul had to say about our hearts:

> Although they knew God, they did not honor him as God
> or give thanks to him, but they became futile in their

thinking, and their *foolish hearts were darkened.* . . . They were filled with all manner of unrighteousness, evil, covetousness, malice. They are full of envy, murder, strife, deceit, maliciousness. They are gossips, slanderers, haters of God, insolent, haughty, boastful, inventors of evil, disobedient to parents, foolish, faithless, heartless, ruthless. (Rom. 1:21, 29–31, emphasis mine)

So no, I don't think it's necessarily wise to follow your heart.

The whole notion of "Be true to yourself" is similarly problematic. Society pounds this idea into us in the unrelenting echo chamber of television, movies, and social media. And it is one of the underlying themes of most movies, even children's movies. Again, "yourself" in this scenario is corrupted by sin, so why be true to that? The whole idea of this is bound to the exaltation of self. It carries the implication of making yourself your own god. Putting yourself and your desires on a pedestal and worshiping them. Being true to yourself is nothing short of idolatry. Oh, and isn't a child molester just being true to himself? A rapist? A thief? A greedy person? And on it goes. So no thank you. I don't want to be true to myself. I want to be true to God and his Word.

CAN YOU BE GAY AND CHRISTIAN?

This one is complex, so let's break it down. First, we must define what we mean by *gay.* If you mean *continuously and unrepentantly engaging in homosexual behavior*, then no, you cannot be a gay Christian. But if you mean *having a same-sex orientation but not acting on that impulse*, then yes, you can be gay and a Christian.

However, I would never call myself a gay Christian, because the label "gay" is part of my old self, which the apostle Paul told us to get rid of: "*Put off your old self*, which belongs to your former manner of life and is corrupt through deceitful desires, and . . . be renewed in the spirit of your minds, and . . . *put on the new self*, created after the likeness of God in true righteousness and holiness" (Eph. 4:22–24, emphasis mine).

I don't identify with that old lifestyle anymore. I am now a new creation in Christ. That old man has passed away (2 Cor. 5:17). In Romans 6:2, Paul gets right to the point: "How can we who died to sin still live in it?" I have died to that old life. That's not who I am anymore, so why would I use the adjective "gay" to describe myself? Some Christians choose to refer to themselves in this way, but I just find the terminology misleading.

This is the way I address the issue if I'm asked about my sexuality: "I am a follower of Christ who happens to experience same-sex attraction." Other Christians may struggle with all kinds of sin: gossip, greed, anger, pride, and so on. But I seriously doubt that they would identify themselves as a "greedy" Christian or a "gossiping" Christian. So why would I identify as a "gay" Christian? The temptation to use this language is understandable. Over the last forty years in our culture, homosexuality has gone from a *behavior* to a full-blown *identity*. This is why we see gay pride parades but not greed pride parades.

Martin Luther famously said that the entire life of a believer is to be one of repentance. But how can you repent of something you don't think is wrong? This is where being a practicing homosexual and a Christian simply does not work. Here's what the apostle John had to say:

> No one who abides in him keeps on sinning; no one who keeps on sinning has either seen him or known him. Little children, let no one deceive you. Whoever practices righteousness is righteous, as he is righteous. Whoever makes a practice of sinning is of the devil, for the devil has been sinning from the beginning. The reason the Son of God appeared was to destroy the works of the devil. No one born of God makes a practice of sinning, for God's seed abides in him; and he cannot keep on sinning, because he has been born of God. (1 John 3:6–9)

That seems harsh, but it's the truth.

The writer of the letter to the Hebrews had these haunting words to say:

> If we go on sinning deliberately after receiving the knowledge of the truth, there no longer remains a sacrifice for

sins, but a fearful expectation of judgment, and a fury of fire that will consume the adversaries. Anyone who has set aside the law of Moses dies without mercy on the evidence of two or three witnesses. How much worse punishment, do you think, will be deserved by the one who has trampled underfoot the Son of God, and has profaned the blood of the covenant by which he was sanctified, and has outraged the Spirit of grace? For we know him who said, "Vengeance is mine; I will repay." And again, "The Lord will judge his people." It is a fearful thing to fall into the hands of the living God. (Heb. 10:26–31)

And Paul put it this way in his letter to the Romans:

You also must consider yourselves dead to sin and alive to God in Christ Jesus.

Let not sin therefore reign in your mortal body, to make you obey its passions. Do not present your members to sin as instruments for unrighteousness, but present yourselves to God as those who have been brought from death to life, and your members to God as instruments for righteousness. (Rom. 6:11–13)

Obedience and faith are two sides of the same coin. In the book of Hebrews, "unbelief" and "disobedience" are synonymous. The writer unpacked why the Israelites, who had been freed from captivity in Egypt, were unable to enter the promised land: "To whom did he swear that they would not enter his rest, but to those who were *disobedient*? So we see that they were unable to enter because of *unbelief*" (Heb. 3:18–19, emphasis mine). In these two verses, the writer made it clear that the Israelites did not enter God's rest because of disobedience/unbelief. We see a clear parallel between the two.

My faith in Christ compels me to pursue a life of obedience. The thought of being disobedient to the One who took on himself the penalty of my sin makes me sick. The fleeting pleasures of sin are not worth the agony of grieving the Person I love the most. It is said that there is no one more miserable than a Christian living in sin. I couldn't agree more.

> By faith Moses, when he was grown up, refused to be called the son of Pharaoh's daughter, choosing rather to be mistreated with the people of God than to enjoy the *fleeting pleasures of sin*. He considered the reproach of Christ greater wealth than the treasures of Egypt, for he was looking to the reward. (Heb. 11:24–26, emphasis mine)

Finally, Paul put it bluntly when he said, "Let everyone who names the name of the Lord depart from iniquity" (2 Tim. 2:19).

ARE YOU STRAIGHT NOW?

I get this question a lot. It's a common misconception that if you are gay and become a Christian, you somehow magically become straight. Of course, that can happen. God created the universe; he can heal sexual brokenness in an instant. But sometimes he allows various struggles to persist, because we are being sanctified. These struggles force us to press into him more and more and depend on his grace to get us "from one degree of glory to another" (2 Cor. 3:18), ultimately conforming us more and more into the image of Christ.

The apostle Paul was no stranger to this kind of adversity. He was given "a thorn . . . in the flesh" (2 Cor. 12:7). We don't know exactly what that thorn was, but that's not the point. We just know that it was his struggle, and he pleaded with God three times to take it away from him. But God said to him, "My grace is sufficient for you, for my power is made perfect in weakness" (2 Cor. 12:9). In Romans 5:3–5, Paul addressed our struggles in a different way:

> We rejoice in our sufferings, knowing that suffering produces endurance, and endurance produces character, and character produces hope, and hope does not put us to shame, because God's love has been poured into our hearts through the Holy Spirit who has been given to us.

My identity is no longer in my sexuality but in Christ. I still struggle with sexual desire for men, but I have to say that after my encounter with Jesus, by the grace of God, that desire has greatly diminished. God may fully heal that sexual broken-ness in me at some point, but for now, I am content simply to be obedient to him. I am more than willing to deny myself, take up my cross, and follow him (Matt. 16:24). He's worth it.

TEN

YOUNG AND RICH

THE TEN-BILLION-DOLLAR BLUNDER

Poor Joe Green. Little did he know that he was walking away from billions of dollars.

Joe Green was Mark Zuckerberg's roommate at Harvard. As schoolmates, Green and Zuckerberg created a website called Facemash, which allowed users to rank fellow Harvard students according to attractiveness. After some outraged students prompted Harvard's administrative board to investigate the controversial website, the board threatened to expel Zuckerberg if he didn't take the website down. Zuckerberg ultimately acquiesced to the board's demands and removed the site.[1]

Facemash may have failed, but it eventually led Zuckerberg to create a little website called Facebook. Zuckerberg dropped out of Harvard his sophomore year to pursue his plans to create a social network. He urged Green to drop out as well and join him on this new venture, offering him shares in Facebook as compensation. But Green's father strongly disapproved and cautioned his son against collaborating with a rogue like Zuckerberg. So he, afraid of disappointing his father, turned down Zuckerberg's offer. Green wasn't willing to risk it all for a potential fortune; he was more concerned with playing it safe. Years later, when Facebook went public, Green's shares would have been worth ten billion dollars![2] Oh well, hindsight is 20/20, right?

THE RICH YOUNG MAN

Joe Green may have lost out on a huge earthly fortune, but the man we're about to meet missed out on something infinitely more valuable: eternal life, "an inheritance that is imperishable, undefiled, and unfading" (1 Peter 1:4). Just like Green, this man was reluctant to risk what he thought made him financially secure, and that reluctance cost him an astonishing inheritance.

In the Synoptic Gospels (the books of Matthew, Mark, and Luke), we are told a powerful story of a rich young man who approached Jesus, who was on his way to Jerusalem. The man asked Jesus a sincere question:

> And as he was setting out on his journey, a man ran up and
> knelt before him and asked him, "Good Teacher, what must

I do to inherit eternal life?" And Jesus said to him, "Why do you call me good? No one is good except God alone. You know the commandments: 'Do not murder, Do not commit adultery, Do not steal, Do not bear false witness, Do not defraud, Honor your father and mother.'" And he said to him, "Teacher, all these I have kept from my youth." And Jesus, looking at him, loved him, and said to him, "You lack one thing: go, sell all that you have and give to the poor, and you will have treasure in heaven; and come, follow me." Disheartened by the saying, he went away sorrowful, for he had great possessions. (Mark 10:17–22)

In his usual fashion, Jesus did not answer this rich young man's question directly. He first challenged him on his assumption that Jesus is good: "No one is good except God alone" (v. 18). In other words, by referring to Jesus as a good teacher, this man showed that he did not believe Jesus is God. So why did he call Jesus good?

In our culture today, we often hear people defend themselves by saying things like, "But I'm a good person." When I shared the gospel with a close friend of mine who is Jewish, her response to the question of whether she was going to heaven was, "Look, I'm a good person. I do the right thing. I'm fine." (Meanwhile, she was having an affair with a married man!) But just as Jesus annihilated that idea here to the rich young man, so did the apostle Paul when he said, "None is righteous, no, not one" (Rom. 3:10).

The idea that we can be good enough that God ought to be pleased with us—even as we knowingly defy his commands—is a human invention without biblical support. Where did we get the idea that God weighs our good and bad deeds on a scale, as though all he wants is for us to do slightly more good than evil? Instead, the Bible carries a relational view of sin: the problem is not that we fail to climb a moral ladder (though we all absolutely do!), it is that our defiance against God's design and commands has broken our relationship with him. And we need him to forgive us and restore that broken relationship, which is exactly what Jesus did.

When the rich young man asked Jesus what he must do to inherit eternal life (Mark 10:17), he was asking how one enters God's kingdom. But this question betrayed the man's assumption that he could somehow earn his way into the kingdom of God, that he could *do* something to get in. Given this assumption, he simply wanted to know what that thing was so he could do it. His question was surely sincere, albeit misguided.

Jesus responded to the man by getting on his level, so to speak. He cited the second tablet of the Ten Commandments (the last five commandments), or the horizontal commandments, as it were, which deals with one's relationship to others. The reason Jesus cited these commandments was probably because they are easier to use to gauge whether one has kept them.[3] The rich man was quick to point out that he had kept all of those commandments since his youth (the age of accountability).

This man certainly seemed to have all his ducks in a row and all the boxes checked . . . or so he thought.

In the passage immediately before this one, Jesus' disciples, who apparently thought they were his Secret Service or something, tried to stop people from bringing their children to him for a blessing. But Jesus rebuked them, saying, "Let the children come to me; do not hinder them, for to such belongs the kingdom of God. Truly, I say to you, whoever does not receive the kingdom of God like a child shall not enter it" (Mark 10:14–15). In other words, one must have childlike faith and dependence on God, rather than self-dependence, to enter his kingdom. The rich young man was focused on his own good works rather than on simply having childlike faith, which is necessary to enter God's kingdom and inherit eternal life.

Jesus exposed the true problem this man was blind to when he said: "You lack one thing: go, sell all that you have and give to the poor, and you will have treasure in heaven; and come, follow me" (Mark 10:21). Using this passage, some have suggested that you cannot be a rich Christian. But that's not what's going on here. Jesus wasn't concerned about the man's wealth; he was concerned about his heart. Jesus knew that the man's heart was set on money, not on God; that he was trying to appease God with his actions, when the only thing God wanted was the man's love.

Jesus exposed what truly mattered to this man, what truly functioned as his god: wealth. It was what he clung to for his identity, what he desired most. Wealth was his idol. But we are told in Luke that "no servant can serve two masters, for either he will hate the one and love the other, or he will be devoted to the one and despise the other. You cannot serve God and money" (Luke 16:13).

So Jesus offered this man the chance to serve the one true Master. He gave him a chance to smash his idol and put God in its place. Jesus told him to go sell everything and follow him, knowing that the man's first love was keeping him from obeying the first and greatest commandment: "love the Lord your God with all your heart and with all your soul and with all your mind" (Matt. 22:37). This perfectly pious man seemed to have it all together, until Jesus challenged his true god.

Now the man had a decision to make: Choose eternal life or the comfort and security of his own wealth? Choose to follow Jesus or to follow the world? Choose life or death? We are told that "Disheartened by the saying, he went away sorrowful, for he had great possessions" (Mark 10:22). He was disheartened because Jesus exposed what was truly in his heart, what he built his identity on. The man left without salvation because of the power his own wealth had over him. He forwent eternal riches for temporal riches. He turned down the kingdom of God for his own little kingdom. Faced with the choice between money and Jesus, he chose money. And, alas, he missed the forest for the trees. This is what is truly very sad.

THE DEAL BREAKER

For the rich young man, wealth was the deal breaker, because it was his identity: "I'm the successful, rich guy. That's who I am." If following Jesus could fit under that heading, everything would have been fine. But when Jesus demanded he let go of his one nonnegotiable in life, it was a deal breaker.

Just as money was the deal breaker for this guy, for many in the LGBT community, their homosexual identity is the deal breaker. It's the hindrance, or stumbling block, that prevents them from even considering following Christ. It certainly was for me for many, many years. As a gay man, I always saw Christians as the enemy. After all, they believe who I am is wrong, even sinful, right?

My Christian family loved me and loved seeing me when I went back to Dallas for the holidays, but underneath it all, I knew they disapproved of my lifestyle. Though they were clearly thrilled to spend time with me, I felt alienated by them and by Christians in general. I just felt like they didn't get me, didn't understand who I was. It was frustrating.

For me personally, becoming a Christian was out of the question. I knew I could never be part of that club, because a fundamental chasm lay between Christianity and my identity as a gay man. There was no crossing over to the other side when they didn't like my kind. And I didn't much care for their kind either. In Los Angeles, I didn't know any Christians and didn't care to. I had my group of open-minded, sexually liberated, and intellectually progressive friends who shielded me from *those* people. Los Angeles provided a safe haven for people like me.

A TALE OF TWO DESTINIES

A gay man in his twenties attended my church in Hollywood for a year with his live-in boyfriend. They came together every Sunday, seemingly unaware (or maybe just wanted to be unaware) that homosexuality is a sin.

They were determined to become disciples of Christ, yet still wanted to hang on to their sinful relationship. But then an amazing thing began to happen. Slowly but surely, one of them, Nathan, began to be convicted by the Holy Spirit. He started to become aware that something was not right about his being in a relationship with another man, while at the same time claiming to be a follower of Jesus. He felt something deep in the recesses of his heart and knew he had to take action.

This was devastating to him because he loved his boyfriend deeply and didn't want to hurt him. It was also painful because he was in love and didn't want the relationship to end. He was facing a very difficult choice. So he decided to meet with our pastor to discuss the issue. Maybe there was a way for him to be a disciple of Christ and still stay with his boyfriend? He hoped that the pastor would give his blessing to the relationship. Times have changed, after all. Maybe he could have both Christ and his boyfriend? But after discussing the matter with the pastor, his hopes were dashed. The pastor showed him that the Bible considers homosexuality a sin and that his relationship was not what God wanted. From there, I was given the opportunity to meet with him and help him continue to work through the situation.

When I met Nathan for coffee, he seemed a bit shaken. His boyfriend was aware that he was meeting with me, and why he was meeting with me. His boyfriend already knew my story and was not happy, to say the least, that he was seeking my advice. But Nathan needed more answers. He wanted more confirmation on this issue, especially from a guy who had been through it, someone who knew where he was coming from.

We had a great conversation. I told him my story and how the gospel totally transformed me, including my thoughts on homosexuality. I explained to him how utterly clear the Bible is on this issue, not just in the so-called clobber passages, in which homosexuality is specifically called out as a sin, but also in the entire scope of the Bible, from Genesis to Revelation. I even used the passage of the rich young man to illustrate the implications of his decision. We ended up talking for several hours.

Near the end of our talk, his phone started blowing up with text messages and phone calls. It was his boyfriend. He was freaking out that Nathan was spending so much time with me. Nathan became distressed at the barrage of texts and calls and told me he needed to go and comfort his boyfriend. But

I urged him to come to the evening church service with me instead, because I thought he needed to be with other believers right then. Nevertheless, he insisted on going back to his boyfriend. So afterwards, I went to church and he went home.

I arrived at church ten minutes later and immediately grabbed a group of brothers and sisters in Christ to pray for Nathan. Just as we were finishing our prayers, my phone rang. It was Nathan. I immediately picked up. He was sobbing. He said in his agitated state he had gotten on the wrong entrance to the freeway, which, instead of taking him back home to the Westside, brought him east, toward the church. I again urged him to come to church and be around believers. This time, he acquiesced.

When he arrived home after the two-hour church service, he discovered that his boyfriend, unable to face what he anticipated Nathan was going to do, had taken all his belongings and moved out. That day they broke up for good. Since then, Nathan has been walking faithfully with the Lord. He quit his real estate job in Los Angeles and is now attending Dallas Theological Seminary. Unlike the rich young man, Nathan gave up the one thing that was keeping him from entering the kingdom of God. He decided that following Christ was more important to him than the fleeting pleasures of sin.

Lucas was a different story. He and I were acquaintances for many years and were friends on Facebook. After my conversion to Christianity, I would occasionally post Bible verses or other Christian writings on Facebook. I noticed that Lucas, a gay man, was "liking" many of my gospel-related posts. I was pleasantly surprised by this, especially because I knew that he was not only gay but also in a serious, live-in relationship with another man, a successful television writer. Eventually, I reached out and invited him to my church. He accepted, much to my shock and joy. When we met up a couple of Sundays later at the church, he said he had enjoyed the service and was impressed by the sermon; he even expressed interest in coming back.

I didn't hear from him for a few weeks though. I was a bit disappointed, but I didn't want to push. With patience, I continued to pray for him. About a month later, I ran into him at an upscale furniture store he owned in West Hollywood, where I was looking for things I needed for a set design job. He greeted me enthusiastically, and we ended up chatting for a while. I told him he was welcome to come back to church any time. But as soon as I mentioned this, his demeanor shifted, and his face fell. He said he was concerned about my church's views on homosexuality. Apparently, he hadn't been aware that my church holds the orthodox view that homosexuality is a sin. I briefly explained why my church follows the biblical view on this, but he wasn't receptive. When I boldly urged him to choose Christ over his sexual identity, he became flustered. I could tell he was torn. I explained to him what was at stake. But he asked how he could be expected to give up such a nice life with his boyfriend.

When I asked him to continue thinking through what we

had talked about, he just nodded. That was five years ago, and I haven't heard from him since. I know he is still in the same relationship. Lucas, like the rich young man, has chosen (as far as I know) something that is more important to him than Christ. He counted the cost and decided not to deny himself. I'm still praying for him.

Before going to church that September day, I was willing, by God's grace, to put my homosexual identity on the shelf and walk in with an open mind and heart. It was as if Jesus were asking me, "Are you willing to forsake romantic relationships with men and follow me?" I must have been, because here I am.

I became like a child as I entered the church, sincerely and humbly seeking God. And God met me there.

ELEVEN

BAD SOUP

If you give your soul up to anything earthly, whether it be the wealth, or the honours, or the pleasures of this world, you might as well hunt after the mirage of the desert or try to collect the mists of the morning, or to store up for yourself the clouds of the sky, for all these things are passing away.

—Charles Haddon Spurgeon

A ROYAL SCANDAL

If you've watched the Netflix hit *The Crown*, you are more or less familiar with this story. On December 11, 1936, a royal scandal of epic proportions erupted in Britain, one that stunned the world even more so than Brexit. In a worldwide radio broadcast, the king of England, Edward VIII, announced his abdication.

After reigning for less than a year, he gave up his title as king of Britain and of the whole British Empire, which included over 500 million subjects, so he could marry the twice-divorced American woman Wallis Simpson. He had fallen deeply in love with her prior to his ascent to the throne, which occurred upon the death of his father, George V. At that time, the Church of England was opposed to the remarriage of divorced people if their spouses were still alive. When Edward abdicated, not only were both of Simpson's husbands living, but she was still married to her second husband, Ernest Simpson. The fact that she was an American didn't help matters either; British royalty were not supposed to marry American commoners. And Prime Minister Stanley Baldwin was against this unorthodox marriage and would have resigned if King Edward had gone through with it. Edward had a decision to make: not marry the love of his life, marry her against the wishes of the prime minister, or abdicate. He chose to abdicate. He gave up *everything* for her, including his birthright as king of England! He was willing to forgo all his royal inheritance for a passion he desired more. He and Simpson married soon after he abdicated.

In the 1920s and 1930s, Edward had been the world's most eligible bachelor. He had a well-known reputation as a womanizer; his exploits included affairs with a Parisian courtesan and several married women. Edward indulged his lusts and passions with reckless abandon. His own father, King George V, was horrified by his son's behavior and hoped he would never become king, even though Edward was next in line for the throne. Edward remained a bachelor throughout his twenties and thirties, until he finally met his match in Simpson.

Once Edward abdicated, his younger brother, Albert, took over as king. For the rest of his life, Edward would be reduced to having to ask for an allowance from Albert, or King George VI as he was later called. Edward essentially went from king to beggar overnight, all because of a passion he couldn't resist. He and Simpson lived in exile in France and elsewhere on borrowed money for the rest of their lives. They were never allowed back in England, except during World War II and upon their respective deaths. Edward died at his home in Paris on May 28, 1972. He was finally allowed to return to England . . . in a casket.[1]

ESAU SELLS HIS BIRTHRIGHT

In Genesis, we find a story with themes similar to that of King Edward VIII's, but with much more dire and tragic consequences. The story of Jacob and Esau, twin sons of Isaac and Rebekah, and grandsons of Abraham, is fraught with complications from the very beginning, when they seemed to be fighting in their mother's womb[2]: "The children struggled together within her" (Gen. 25:22).

Rebekah finally conceived after having been barren for the first twenty years of her marriage. But her pregnancy was so painful that she wondered if there was any point in living.[3] Even the delivery was difficult. Jacob followed Esau, grabbing Esau's heel as he came out of the womb, as if he were trying to pull Esau back into the womb so he could be the firstborn son and inherit all the privileges that came with it.[4] This struggle between the two sons would continue to play out as they got older.

As teenagers, they were quite opposite in disposition: Esau, an outdoorsy man's man, liked to hunt, while the domestic Jacob was happy to stay at home.[5] Esau was favored by his father, Isaac, because he had a taste for the game Esau would bring home, while Jacob was preferred by his doting mother, Rebekah (Gen. 25:28). They were as different as two brothers could be. But then, an incident occurred between the two boys that would have everlasting consequences:

Once when Jacob was cooking stew, Esau came in from the field, and he was exhausted. And Esau said to Jacob, "Let me eat some of that red stew, for I am exhausted!" (Therefore his name was called Edom.) Jacob said, "Sell me your birthright now." Esau said, "I am about to die; of what use is a birthright to me?" Jacob said, "Swear to me now." So he swore to him and sold his birthright to Jacob. Then Jacob gave Esau bread and lentil stew, and he ate and drank and rose and went his way. Thus Esau despised his birthright. (Gen. 25:29–34)

When the pragmatic and coarse Esau walked in the house, famished and exhausted from hunting, he not only wanted what Jacob had but wanted it right then and there that he readily gave up his birthright. And Jacob, still grabbing at Esau's heel, as it were, took advantage of his brother's weakness and tricked him into giving up his birthright. Ravenous and impulsive, Esau was all too amenable to this wildly imbalanced quid pro quo; lentils were common, but a birthright was unmatched.[6] When he said he was "about to die" (v. 32), he was probably using hyperbole, in the same way we might say, "I'm starving to death!" even though we had lunch just a few hours ago.[7] It's a bit ironic that Esau, "a skillful hunter" (v. 27), must beg his brother for food. Unfortunately for Esau, he left the encounter with a full stomach, while Jacob left with the much more valuable birthright.

But let's take a step back and examine what was really going on here. Why did Jacob want Esau's birthright? What does birthright even mean? To our twenty-first-century Westerner ears, this word means very little, if anything at all. No one really cares about birth order—or the gender of the baby, for that matter. Being the firstborn has no particular significance in our culture. If anything, the firstborn gets a raw deal, because he or she usually has to be the guinea pig for new, nervous helicopter parents. As the youngest of eight children, I can testify that it was extremely beneficial to have had seven older siblings who wore out my parents before they got to me. By the time I was in high school, my parents no longer even knew how to say the word "curfew." But in ancient cultures, being the firstborn male was everything.

The term *birthright* refers to the rights of the firstborn male. This son held a position of honor and privilege in the family, as well as a double portion of his father's inheritance, which was split into as many portions as he had sons. For example, if the father had nine sons, the firstborn son would receive two portions of the inheritance, while the other eight would split the remaining seven portions. This meant that in the case of two sons, as was the case with Jacob and Esau, the firstborn inherited two-thirds of the inheritance.[8] More important, as Abraham's grandson, Esau was to inherit the Abrahamic covenant, with its three promises:

1. *Personal blessing:* He would be the father of a great nation and many other nations (Gen. 12:2, 13:16, 15:5, 17:6), and he would be blessed and have a great name (Gen. 12:2–3).

2. *National blessing:* A great nation would come from him (Gen. 12:2, 13:16, 15:5), and through him the nation would receive a land to be its homeland forever (Gen. 15:18–21, 17:7–8), as well as the seed to constitute this nation (Gen. 15:2–4).

3. *Universal blessing:* Salvation through him would spread to the ends of the earth: "In you all the families of the earth shall be blessed" (Gen. 12:3).[9]

"To possess the divine birthright and be part of this chosen seed was the greatest blessing any one could hope to receive."[10] Wow. Yet Esau forfeited all that simply for some fast food, because he had to have his meal *now*. "Their end is destruction, their god is their belly, and they glory in their shame, with minds set on earthly things" (Phil. 3:19). Esau lived only for the moment; he couldn't wait until the wedding feast (Matt. 22:1–14; Rev. 19:9). He cared more about the present than the future.

Jacob gave Esau the lentil stew, which Esau happily took and ate. This is reminiscent of the scene in the garden of Eden: "So when the woman saw that the tree was good for food, and that it was a delight to the eyes . . . she took of its fruit and ate, and she also gave some to her husband who was with her, and he ate" (Gen. 3:6). We know the consequences of this monumental transgression. Notice that immediately after Esau satisfied his appetite, he got up and left. He had no remorse for what he had just given up; he had no regret. His actions betrayed his contempt for his birthright (Gen. 25:34).

Esau and Edward VIII were cut from the same cloth: Both were willing to forgo a kingdom that was rightfully theirs for a fleeting indulgence. Both had contempt, not only for their position, but also for their parents.[11] And just as Edward VIII begged for reentry into Britain but was refused, so Esau begged for his father's blessing but was rejected. Both lived to regret their mistake after it was too late.

SELLING YOUR BIRTHRIGHT FOR SEX

I have a friend who grew up in a Christian home with amazing Christian parents. They raised him "in the discipline and instruction of the Lord" (Eph. 6:4). At a young age, he put his trust in Christ as his Lord and Savior, and his faith was vital and flourishing in his life. When he was eighteen years old, he went off to an evangelical Christian university, where his faith continued to grow. But as time went on, his feelings and attractions toward the same sex became more and more evident in his mind and heart. These feelings alarmed and confused him, since he knew and believed what the Bible had to say about homosexuality; as his feelings increased, so did his inner turmoil. He was torn between the sexual ethic laid out in the Bible and his same-sex attractions.

He hid his struggle from others, especially from his parents, during his college years. But feeling ashamed and even hopeless at times, he sought help, and eventually opened up to close friends and even his parents. Reactions were mixed. His parents were initially distraught, but soon became more and more compassionate and understanding. They hoped he would remain faithful to the Word of God and wanted to be there for him in any way they could. Some of his friends rejected him, while others tried to help him through this difficult and confusing period.

After college, he seemed to be in a good place with the Lord. He felt like he had a handle on things and was willing to deny himself to follow Christ. But then, his Wallis Simpson, his lentil stew, entered the picture. He met a guy and fell in love. Although he was torn about this new relationship, knowing it was wrong, he had never felt so good and free. And his boyfriend assured him over and over again that their relationship was not sinful. How could love this deep be sinful? Wasn't the Bible outdated when it came to these matters? He just needed to be true to himself, and everything would work out fine.

My friend ultimately gave in to his feelings, and to his boyfriend's pleas, and made a conscious decision to walk away from the Lord and pursue this relationship. He knew deep down that living a homosexual life was incompatible with the teaching of the Bible, but he was tired of fighting his desires. He wanted his stew now.

As a Christian, I've seen this phenomenon over and over again, and it breaks my heart. I've watched many who profess to be followers of Christ give up their birthright for a single meal, choosing their desire to satiate their appetite now over the amazing promises of Christ. When I talk to young people who struggle with same-sex attraction and are about to throw in the towel and give in to that temptation, I try to help them see what a vapor this life is. Funny as it sounds, I try to make them understand that eternity is a very long time. I try to convince them that selling their birthright is not worth it. I always reference these powerful verses:

> This light momentary affliction is preparing for us an eternal weight of glory beyond all comparison, as we look not

to the things that are seen but to the things that are unseen.
For the things that are seen are transient, but the things
that are unseen are eternal. (2 Cor. 4:17–18)

These verses are always a salve to the soul when I struggle
with temptation. (Yes, I still do!) I need only to remember
the wedding feast, and everything else evaporates. It's hard to
fathom the eternal weight of glory, but I know it is infinitely
more gratifying than any ephemeral pleasure on this earth.
Matthew Henry says of Esau's tragic decision, "The gratifying
of the sensual appetite is that which ruins thousands of pre-
cious souls."[12]

In the New Testament, the writer of Hebrews made a chilling reference to the fate of Esau:

See to it . . . that no one is sexually immoral or unholy
like Esau, who sold his birthright for a single meal. For
you know that afterward, when he desired to inherit the
blessing, he was rejected, for he found no chance to repent,
though he sought it with tears. (Heb. 12:15–17)

Although Esau sold his birthright, he later changed his mind
and wanted his father's blessing. The blessing from Isaac
would have restored his inheritance of "divine potency, pros-
perity, and dominion."[13]

But it was too late.

ESAU AND *THE PILGRIM'S PROGRESS*

In John Bunyan's famous allegory, *The Pilgrim's Progress*, we see a similar theme with a character called "a man in an iron *Cage*." On the road to the celestial city, the central character, Christian, meets this sad man in a dark room in a beautiful, stately palace. Christian asks the man who he is, and he responds:

> I was once a fair and flourishing professor [person who professed the faith], both in mine own eyes, and also in the eyes of others: I once was, as I thought, fair for the Celestial City [heaven], and had then even joy at the thoughts that I should get thither [there].[14]

When Christian asks him how he came to this wretched condition, the man goes on to say that he was put there and is unable to get out because:

> I left off to watch, and be sober, I laid the reins upon the neck of my lusts; I sinned against the light of the Word, and the goodness of God: I have grieved the Spirit, and he is gone; I tempted the Devil, and he is come to me; I have provoked God to anger, and he has left me; I have so hardened my heart, that I *cannot* repent.[15]

Christian asks if there is any hope, and the man responds:

> No, none at all. I have crucified him to myself afresh, I have despised his righteousness, I have counted his blood an unholy thing, I have done despite to the spirit of grace: therefore I have shot myself out of all the promises, and there now remains to me nothing but threatenings, dreadful threatenings, faithful threatenings, of certain judgement and fiery indignation, which shall devour me as an adversary.[16]

Christian then asks him, "For what did you bring yourself into this condition?" The man answered:

> For the lusts, pleasures, and profits of this world; in the enjoyment of which, I did then promise myself much delight: but now every one of those things bite me, and gnaw me like a burning worm.[17]

What a chilling cautionary tale. How dangerous it is to take God's grace for granted and mess with the Holy Spirit. I don't want to live my life challenging God at every turn by staying just on the edge of sin. I want to be completely obedient to my Father, not only because of the great love with which he loved me, but because of the amazing grace he showed me. As Tim Keller says, "I obey because I am accepted through Christ by God."[18] I obey because I am an heir of God and a fellow heir with Christ (Rom. 8:17). God adopted me into his kingdom when I was born again. Why would I ever want to sell that birthright? I cherish my birthright. Nothing in this world is worth trading for that incredible gift from God.

WHATEVER HAPPENED TO ESAU?

Later in Genesis, we learn that God changed Jacob's name to Israel (Gen.32:28). We know from earlier in Genesis that Esau's name was also Edom (Gen. 25:30). It is said that the Israelites (the line from Jacob) and the Edomites (the line from Esau) would be adversaries for hundreds of years. In fact, over four hundred years later, it was the Edomites who denied the Israelites, who had been wandering in the desert for forty years after their exodus from Egypt, to pass through their territory (the fastest route[19]) into Canaan, the promised land (Num. 20:18). Even though these two nations were descendants of the twin brothers, the Edomites had contempt for Israel, just as Esau had contempt for his birthright and his brother Jacob. So here we have it: Esau, who sold his birthright for a single meal, not only rejected God, but he also ended up, in effect, rejecting God's chosen people.

The first chapter of the gospel of Matthew begins with a genealogy from Abraham all the way to Jesus. I know it may seem like a tedious passage to read through, but just bear with me and take a look at the list of names mentioned:

The book of the genealogy of Jesus Christ, the son of David, the son of Abraham.

Abraham was the father of *Isaac,* and Isaac the father of *Jacob,* and Jacob the father of Judah and his brothers, and Judah the father of Perez and Zerah by Tamar, and Perez the father of Hezron, and Hezron the father of Ram, and Ram the father of Amminadab, and Amminadab the father of Nahshon, and Nahshon the father of Salmon, and Salmon the father of Boaz by Rahab, and Boaz the father of Obed by Ruth, and Obed the father of Jesse, and Jesse the father of *David* the king.

And David was the father of Solomon by the wife of Uriah, and Solomon the father of Rehoboam, and Rehoboam the father of Abijah, and Abijah the father of Asaph, and Asaph the father of Jehoshaphat, and Jehoshaphat the father of Joram, and Joram the father of Uzziah, and Uzziah the father of Jotham, and Jotham the father of Ahaz, and Ahaz the father of Hezekiah, and Hezekiah the father of Manasseh, and Manasseh the father of Amos, and Amos the father of Josiah, and Josiah the father of Jechoniah and his brothers, at the time of the deportation to Babylon.

And after the deportation to Babylon: Jechoniah was the father of Shealtiel, and Shealtiel the father of

Zerubbabel, and Zerubbabel the father of Abiud, and Abiud the father of Eliakim, and Eliakim the father of Azor, and Azor the father of Zadok, and Zadok the father of Achim, and Achim the father of Eliud, and Eliud the father of Eleazar, and Eleazar the father of Matthan, and Matthan the father of Jacob, and Jacob the father of Joseph the husband of Mary, of whom *Jesus* was born, who is called Christ. (Matt. 1:1–16, emphasis mine)

What name is glaringly missing from this long list of the key names in God's epic plan of salvation? *Esau.* The silence is deafening. It's downright haunting. Though Esau was the firstborn son of Isaac, his name is not listed here because he chose to give up his birthright to satisfy his hunger; he gave up his place on this list for a crummy meal. John Calvin puts it in stark terms: "It would have been his true wisdom rather to undergo a thousand deaths than to renounce his birthright."[20]

There will come a day when we will meet Christ face-to-face. That day will be either the greatest or the most devastating day imaginable, depending on whether or not your name is written in the Book of Life: "If anyone's name was not found written in the book of life, he was thrown into the lake of fire" (Rev. 20:15). There could be nothing more frightening than to have your name not be on that list. What do you want to hear on that day? "Well done, good and faithful servant" (Matt. 25:21)? Or, "I never knew you; depart from me" (Matt. 7:23)? The latter is the most terrifying words a human being could ever hear. What would you be willing to give up to avoid that outcome? What would you refuse to do if it meant spending eternity with Christ?

Let us "deny [ourselves] and take up [our] cross and follow [him]" (Matt. 16:24). Let us "fight the good fight of the faith" and "take hold of the eternal life to which [we] were called and about which [we] made the good confession in the presence of many witnesses" (1 Tim. 6:12). Let us "run with endurance the race that is set before us" (Heb. 12:1). Let us, "as obedient children, . . . not be conformed to the passions of [our] former ignorance, but as he who called [us] is holy . . . be holy in all [our] conduct, since it is written, 'You shall be holy, for I am holy'" (1 Peter 1:14–16). Let us "hold fast the confession of our hope without wavering" (Heb. 10:23).

The only true passion to live this life for is the passion for Christ. The only true meal is the Bread of Life. The only true drink is the water that will never make us thirsty again—the living water of Christ.

TWELVE

THREE GUYS
AND A FURNACE

The time is coming when people will not endure sound teaching, but having itching ears they will accumulate for themselves teachers to suit their own passions.

—2 TIMOTHY 4:3

By pretending to have transcended particular narratives and discovered the archetypal truth in itself, we forget that many of our most cherished values, expectations, and convictions are creations of a particular time and place rather than universal truths.

—JEAN-FRANÇOIS LYOTARD, PARAPHRASED BY
MICHAEL HORTON IN *THE CHRISTIAN FAITH*

Homosexuality is one of the most highly charged issues of the day. It touches every aspect of contemporary life: families, community, the media, politics, and even the church. Not a day goes by that I don't see several stories or op-ed pieces in the *New York Times* regarding this issue, and many of them prominently. The massive attention the LGBT community is getting in the media is unprecedented, and its influence on the church has been profound.

Some of my close Christian friends who I thought were deeply committed to the authority of Scripture, and who held firmly to the belief that homosexuality is a sin, have recently done an about-face on the issue. A friend I've known for eight years, who was always super "on fire" for the Lord, and by all appearances was a mature and strong Christian, recently posted a video on Facebook endorsing homosexuality. Not only did it shock me that she so quickly changed her position, but it also very personally pained me to see this happen.

Many Christians, especially young ones, are being pressured into this notion that it is more loving to affirm homosexuality. It might seem like a good idea. After all, Christ loved the woman caught in adultery, right? What believers and nonbelievers alike invariably fail to remember about that story is its ending, where Jesus told the woman, "From now on *sin no more*" (John 8:11, emphasis mine).

Posting gay-affirming statements on social media might make my friend seem more loving toward the LGBT community, but it's actually quite deadly and destructive. She bought the lie but doesn't yet know that what she bought is a fake. In the meantime, she's selling the lie to other hapless and gullible Christians. How did she get to this point? How did her views shift so dramatically? To what extent did the culture she lives in make this decision for her? Let's take a look at one particular story in Scripture to help us better grasp the importance of holding fast to God's Word and resisting the influence and demands of the world around us.

In the book of Daniel in the Old Testament, we find a riveting tale of God's people exiled in a foreign land. This famous story of faithfulness in the midst of severe trial is familiar to most Christians. Daniel and his friends Shadrach, Meshach, and Abednego were captives in the hostile nation of Babylon, whose king was none other than the tyrannical Nebuchadnezzar. In 605 BC, Nebuchadnezzar invaded Jerusalem and besieged the capital city of Judah. He then ordered one of his chief court officials, Ashpenaz, to bring some of the best and brightest of the Jews to Babylon to teach them the language and literature of the Chaldeans (Babylonians).[1] They were to be of noble birth and "youths without blemish, of good appearance and skillful in all wisdom" (Dan. 1:4). In other words, these young men needed to be smart, good looking, and pedigreed. Apparently, Daniel and his friends fit this description.

In ordering them to study the literature of the Babylonian culture, Nebuchadnezzar was not just asking them to read a few books. During their three-year reeducation period, these four young Jewish men were given new names (identity) and placed on a new diet.[2] The goal was to totally reorient their thoughts, beliefs, and practices to that of this pagan nation[3]; in other words, "to obliterate all memory of Israel and Israel's God from the lips and minds of these young men, and to instill into them a sense of total dependence on Nebuchadnezzar for all of the good things in life."[4] After this reprogramming, these young men would be ready to enter into the king's service (Dan. 1:5).

Daniel and his friends submitted to the authority of Nebuchadnezzar and did as they were told, but only to a certain point. Some things were not up for compromise[5]: "Daniel *resolved* that he would not defile himself with the king's food, or with the wine that he drank" (Dan. 1:8, emphasis mine). Notice that Daniel immediately drew a line in the Babylonian sand. His conscience and convictions would not allow for certain accommodations. It's not clear from the text exactly why Daniel refused to partake in the king's food and wine, but he most likely didn't want to indulge in the king's luxuries in an effort to avoid being ensnared by the comforts of this alien land.[6] Daniel ended up getting his way on this matter, but not on other matters of contention that arise later in this story.

A couple of chapters later, we find Daniel's friends, Shadrach, Meshach, and Abednego, taking the heat for standing up for their beliefs and not bowing down to Nebuchadnezzar's demands. The not-so-subtle and egomaniacal Nebuchadnezzar decided to build a ninety-foot-high, nine-foot-wide[7] golden statue. It remains unclear whether this statue was an image of Nebuchadnezzar or of some deity in the Babylonian pantheon.[8] Regardless, this statue was both a way to establish a lasting testimony to Nebuchadnezzar's glory and a means to unify his kingdom.[9] All the royal administrators of the provinces, representing the many peoples, nations, and languages of Nebuchadnezzar's wide domain, were to attend the dedication of the statue and, at the sound of music playing from the myriad instruments, were to *bow down* to this giant gilded idol—or die! "Whoever does not fall down and worship shall immediately be cast into a burning fiery furnace" (Dan. 3:6). This threat of capital punishment by fire was no joke; burning was a well-attested punishment for criminals in ancient Babylonia.[10]

But there was one small problem for the three: God's Word, revealed to them through Moses in what we call the Ten Commandments, prohibited the worshiping of idols:

> You shall have no other gods before me.
>
> You shall not make for yourself a *carved image*, or any likeness of anything that is in heaven above, or that is in the earth beneath, or that is in the water under the earth. You *shall not bow down* to them or serve them, for I the LORD your God am a jealous God. (Ex. 20:3–5, emphasis mine)

They knew God's Word, and his Word was clear. So they chose to stand against the demands of their new society and remain faithful to God.

Before long, some of the Babylonian authorities, who resented the three young men's prominence in *their* government, informed Nebuchadnezzar of their refusal to bow down and worship the golden image. "They were inflamed with jealousy," according to John Calvin.[11] How dare these three foreigners, these Jewish *captives*, not obey the directive of their king! Who did they think they were? The report of this insubordination sent Nebuchadnezzar into a rage, and Shadrach, Meshach, and Abednego were summoned before him. He demanded to know if the accusations were true. Did they in fact refuse to bow down and worship the golden image? Did they remember that the fiery furnace was waiting for them if they gave the wrong answer?

Their response is fascinating. Cool as kosher cucumbers, they calmly and confidently informed Nebuchadnezzar that they "have no need to answer [him] in this matter" (Dan. 3:16). They did not fear man, not even one of the most powerful despots in the ancient world![12] Their convictions were set. They were not interested in compromising God's Word; they were interested in God's glory. God's glory was much more important to them than even their own lives.[13]

They knew well from their own history that their God could deliver them from the blazing furnace, just as he had delivered their ancestors from bondage in Egypt. But even if God chose not to spare them from a fiery death, they would hold the line. This episode brings to mind Jesus' words in the gospel of Matthew: "Do not fear those who kill the body but cannot kill the soul. Rather fear him who can destroy both soul and body in hell" (Matt. 10:28). These men were not afraid of mere physical death, because they understood that spiritual death was much more frightening.

Of course, their response enraged Nebuchadnezzar even more, and he "ordered the furnace heated seven times more than it was usually heated" (Dan. 3:19). He also had some of his strongest soldiers bind and cast them into the fiery furnace. These "mighty men" (Dan. 3:20) who cast them into the furnace were immediately burnt to a crisp because of the extreme heat, but much to the shock and amazement of Nebuchadnezzar, the three friends were completely unharmed; not even a hair on their heads was singed.

To make matters even more incredible, there was a fourth mystery man in the furnace with them. There's a debate among scholars on who this fourth figure could be. Was he God? An angel? Whoever he was, God clearly showed that he cared for his believers in distress. "God did not simply rescue them from the fire, but he sent his personal emissary to pass through the fire with them."[14] Wow. What an amazing testimony to God's power and love!

We find a similar story of courage under fire when Martin Luther was ordered to appear before the Holy Roman Emperor Charles V at the Diet of Worms and recant his belief in the doctrine of justification by faith alone. Luther held fast to his convictions, despite facing the fire of imminent arrest and punishment. When asked to recant, Luther famously responded:

> Unless I am convinced by the testimony of the Scriptures
> or by clear reason . . . my conscience is captive to the Word
> of God. I cannot and will not recant anything, since it is
> neither safe nor right to go against conscience. May God
> help me. Amen.[15]

By the grace of God and with the help of his local ruler, Frederick the Wise of Saxony, Luther was able to escape the Edict of Worms, which called for his capture and punishment.

Like Shadrach, Meshach, and Abednego, Luther refused to compromise when it came to God's Word, as his conscience was "captive to the Word of God." The consciences of today's Christians are being corrupted by the oppressive cultural milieu and the extreme social pressure surrounding the issue of homosexuality. But we know that the law of the Lord is written on our hearts (Jer. 31:31–33), and though we may succeed in muting our conscience, the Word of God is eternal: "The grass withers, the flower fades, but the word of our God will stand forever" (Isa. 40:8). It is never *safe* to tamper with conscience, and it is absolutely *fatal* to tamper with God's Word.

Satan tampered with God's Word in the garden, twisting it just enough for Eve to buy it, and look where that got us! Of course, Satan is still in the business of twisting God's Word today. Just as he questioned Eve, "Did God *actually* say, 'You shall not eat of any tree in the garden'?" (Gen. 3:1, emphasis mine), so, too, is he craftily at work today questioning Christians, "Did God *actually* say homosexuality is a sin?

Sure, his Word mentions it a handful of times, but surely that was just a cultural taboo at the time, right? Besides, all the prohibitions in the Bible regarding homosexuality were not really aimed at the contemporary notion of sexual *orientation*. The biblical authors were not forbidding all same-sex relationships, but only exploitative ones—pederasty, prostitution, and rape, right?"[16]

This is the radical revision of Christianity's stance on this issue, a revision that has developed in the recent past. And Christians today are buying this lie hook, line, and sinker. We ignore the apostle Peter's warning:

> False prophets also arose among the people, just as there will be false teachers among you, who will secretly bring in destructive heresies, even denying the Master who bought them, bringing upon themselves swift destruction. *And many will follow their sensuality, and because of them the way of truth will be blasphemed.* (2 Peter 2:1–2, emphasis mine)

The apostle Paul also delivered a similar warning: "The time is coming when people will not endure sound teaching, but having itching ears they will accumulate for themselves teachers *to suit their own passions*" (2 Tim. 4:3, emphasis mine). As the prophet Elijah asked, "How long will you go limping between two different opinions?" (1 Kings 18:21).

In 1 Peter 5:8, the apostle Peter exhorted Christians, "Be

sober-minded; be watchful. Your adversary the devil prowls around like a roaring lion, seeking someone to devour." Satan is devouring many victims as our culture continues to celebrate homosexuality as a sacrament rather than a sin. And he is even devouring Christians who celebrate this sin alongside the culture. He couldn't be more pleased with his handiwork. "The prince of the power of the air" (Eph. 2:2) is winning this battle at the moment, but he will lose the war in the end. He will be crushed for good (Rev. 20:10).

What if what happened to Daniel and his friends happened to you? What if you were ripped from your environment and placed in a society with new cultural norms? What if that culture was foisted upon you through force or coercion and you were required to compromise some of your convictions? In many ways, this is what is happening now to all of us who profess Christ. We are exiles in this world. "Beloved, I urge you as sojourners and *exiles*" (1 Peter 2:11, emphasis mine).

In the famous "Hall of Faith" passage in the letter to the Hebrews, the author recounted the faith by which the great men and women in the Old Testament lived (Heb. 11). He also noted their alien status in this world: "These all died in faith, not having received the things promised, but having seen them and greeted them from afar, and having acknowledged that *they were strangers and exiles on the earth*" (Heb. 11:13, emphasis mine). He went on to say that "they desire a better country, that is, a heavenly one" (Heb. 11:16). So here we are, as aliens, sojourners, and strangers in this world, waiting for a better world that is to come. But what does this exile look like?

True Christians in the West are by default becoming more and more distinct from the surrounding culture. As the culture quickly slips into neo-paganism, proclaiming Christ is becoming more and more dangerous and offensive. This can have a devastating effect on our relationships, our reputations, and even our jobs. As a production designer in Los Angeles, I've seen this in action. A few years ago, I was working on a fashion shoot at one of the most prestigious photo studios in town. In another studio in the same building, a high-end fashion shoot was in full swing. When the photographer, a gay man, discovered that one of the male models was a Christian, he promptly had him fired. He made it clear that Christians were not welcome on his set. Being a Christian cost this model his job!

Claiming the name of Christ is sometimes a dangerous business. And holding to God's revealed truth in his Word concerning homosexuality is even more dangerous. If you believe that homosexuality is a sin, you are immediately labeled a bigot or homophobic. It's not even okay anymore to just agree to disagree. How did this happen? How did the hostility become so fiery? Somewhere in the last decade, "I disagree with you" came to mean "I hate you." *Tolerance* used to mean something along the lines of, "I disagree with your view, but I'm willing to tolerate it," because it wouldn't be tolerance otherwise. Now, however, tolerance has been redefined as,

"If you don't affirm *everything* I do, then you are intolerant!" What a stunning reversal.

But that's exactly what the culture is telling us today. We'd better get with the program, or we'll be shamed one way or another: financially, socially, even legally. *Time* magazine recently published an article titled, "Regular Christians Are No Longer Welcome in American Culture." In it reads, "[W]hen some American citizens are fearful of expressing their religious views, something new has snaked its way into the village square: an insidious intolerance for religion that has no place in a country founded on religious freedom."[17] The more the LGBT community comes out of the closet, the more Christians are expected to go into the closet. The irony is too absurd to fathom.

Although we are not forced to bow down to a golden image, we are pressured to bow down to the great god of Public Opinion. Over the last several years, I've seen many Christians cave to culture. We are bombarded 24/7 by the news media, literature, television, movies, and social media; even billboards on the streets can influence our thoughts. This happened to me one day as I was driving.

I often listen to the Bible on audio as I drive around Los Angeles, given that the traffic will allow me plenty of time to get through a book or two. Recently, on my hour-long commute from West Hollywood to the seminary in La Mirada, I decided to get through some of the letters in the New Testament. By the time I was heading back to West Hollywood, I had made it through almost all of them. Then, as I was driving up Fairfax Avenue, I noticed a billboard advertising a movie for some goofy, blockbuster comedy. I remember feeling repulsed at the banality and worldliness of it. It wasn't even a particularly raunchy movie, but I had just spent two hours that day immersed in the Word of God, and suddenly the world had no appeal to me. In fact, it repelled me.

I always tell Christians (half-jokingly, but seriously) that for every hour of TV we watch, we must read our Bibles for an hour, because we've just been lied to (implicitly or explicitly) for sixty minutes and need to combat those lies with the truth. As the legendary London preacher, Dick Lucas, once keenly observed, we are either giving in to the pressure of the *world* or giving in to the pressure of the *Word*. As Christians, we are never simply in neutral; we are either being swept downstream by the world or swimming upstream in holiness. There is no state of stasis for a Christian. You are either loving "the Lord your God with all your heart and with all your soul and with all your mind" (Matt. 22:37), or you are loving something or someone else. You are either walking "in the counsel of the wicked" or delighting "in the law of the LORD" (Ps. 1:1–2). You are either being "conformed to this world" or being "transformed by the renewal of your mind" (Rom. 12:2). As it is written in Scripture: "Do you not know that friendship with the world is enmity with God? Therefore whoever wishes to be a friend of the world makes himself an enemy of God" (James 4:4).

That's why Paul correlates the Christian life to that of a soldier in battle and exhorts us to "put on the whole armor of God" every day so we can "stand against the schemes of the devil" (Eph. 6:11). We are engaged in a battle, whether we like it or not. Satan wants nothing more than for us to give in on the issue of homosexuality, because then he can keep more and more people in darkness. He's thrilled that so many Christians have already caved to the pressures of society regarding this issue.

The most dangerous part of this is that if homosexuality were no longer regarded as a sin, then why would anyone need to repent of it? And if there is no repentance, of course, there is no salvation: "Repent therefore, and turn back, that your sins may be blotted out" (Acts 3:19). How can someone be forgiven if they don't repent? It seems unloving to say that homosexuality is a sin, but when we fail to tell someone who is engaging in homosexual behavior the truth that it is sin, we are acting as accomplices to murder. This may sound extreme, but if you aren't truthful, you are knowingly aiding and abetting them down the path of destruction. This is truly the most unloving thing you could do. It has *eternal* consequences.

As Christians, we must be willing to go into the fiery furnace rather than compromise God's Word on the issue of homosexuality. We must be willing to go into the furnace of ridicule from family, friends, and society; the furnace of unpopularity and rejection; the furnace of consternation from colleagues and risk of job loss; and even the furnace of jail, like Andrew Brunson, who was recently released from prison in Turkey after spending two years for the crime of preaching the gospel. It is easy to follow the world but difficult to follow Christ: "Jesus told his disciples, 'If anyone would come after me, let him deny himself and take up his cross and follow me. For whoever would save his life will lose it, but whoever loses his life for my sake will find it. For what will it profit a man if he gains the whole world and forfeits his soul?'" (Matt. 16:24–26).

We are often warned by the world to be on the right side of history. But I'm interested in being on the right side of *God's* history, not of *man's* history. As Christians, we are called to be *in* the world, not *of* the world. As David Wells writes in *God in the Wasteland*, "Worldliness is what makes sin look normal in any age and righteousness seem odd."⁹ We are to be countercultural in those places in which the call and character of God lead us against the grain, even when the stakes are high. But we needn't fear. As with Shadrach, Meshach, and Abednego, God will be with us in the furnace. "Be strong and courageous. Do not fear or be in dread of them, for it is the LORD your God who goes with you. He will not leave you or forsake you" (Deut. 31:6).

Jesus Christ, the Son of God, came into this world, took on flesh, and willingly went into the fiery furnace so we wouldn't have to. He went into the furnace to save us from being thrown into the lake of fire (Rev. 20:15). And there was no other figure with him in that furnace; he was completely and utterly alone and totally abandoned by God. "There was no companion to share his burden, no angel sent to relieve his agony, no saving hand from God stretched down to preserve his faithful servant in his moment of greatest need."[19] Jesus took our place in that furnace—the furnace we deserved—even though he was without sin. He lived the perfect life we should have lived and died the death we should have died for our sins.

Jesus, like the three friends, was faithful, but in his case, unto death. He did all this "for the joy that was set before him" (Heb. 12:2), and that joy was us. In other words, Christ suffered a brutal and violent death so that we could be saved and reconciled to God, for that was his joy: that we may have everlasting fellowship with him. This is good news indeed!

Jesus refused to disobey God when tempted by Satan in the wilderness, even when the temptation was fierce: "Again, the devil took him to a very high mountain and showed him all the kingdoms of the world and their glory. And he said to him, 'All these I will give you, if you will fall down and worship me'" (Matt. 4:8–9). Under this intense pressure, Jesus didn't cave; he resisted the devil, and Satan fled (James 4:7). How did he resist the devil? He used "the sword of the Spirit, which is the word of God" (Eph. 6:17). Jesus responded immediately to Satan with this powerful sword: "Be gone, Satan! For it is written, 'You shall worship the Lord your God and him only shall you serve'" (Matt. 4:10). This sword was at the ready because Jesus *knew* the Scriptures.

In the end, all human beings who have ever existed, of all

"peoples, nations, and languages" (Dan. 3:4), will have to bow down to God. But this time, it won't be to an image of gold but to the true King, Jesus Christ—an indestructible King, an eternal King. And there won't be any choice in the matter: "God has highly exalted him and bestowed on him the name that is above every name, so that at the name of Jesus every knee should bow, in heaven and on earth and under the earth, and every tongue confess that Jesus Christ is Lord" (Phil. 2:9–11).

Let us never forget these words: "Whoever is ashamed of me and of my words, of him will the Son of Man be ashamed when he comes in his glory and the glory of the Father and of the holy angels" (Luke 9:26). Let us never be ashamed of his Word, even when the entire world is telling us that his clear and true Word regarding homosexuality is not to be trusted.

Let us trust in his Word because he is the Word.

THIRTEEN

A CALL TO LOVE

It's the Holy Spirit's job to convict, God's job to judge, and my job to love.

—BILLY GRAHAM

DEAR PASTORS, PARENTS, AND FRIENDS

My desire in this chapter is to impart whatever wisdom I have gleaned over the years as someone who has been on both sides of this thorny issue. Someone who has been called "out of darkness into his marvelous light" (1 Peter 2:9). Someone who was once lost in the homosexual life, without even being aware of it, but by God's grace is now found. Someone who was once not one of God's people but now belongs to his body. And someone who once had not received mercy but now has it (1 Peter 2:10).

My hope is that parents and family members will walk away better equipped to engage their sons and daughters, brothers and sisters, and nieces and nephews who identify as gay or lesbian; and pastors, with those within the body of Christ who struggle with same-sex attraction. What is the best way to come alongside these Christians who are seeking clarity? What is the best way to minister to them? What is the best way to point them to Christ in a *Christlike* way?

I'm not claiming that this is an easy road for anyone involved. In fact, I think homosexuality is one of the most difficult sins to untangle, process, and redeem. Homosexual orientation affects the whole person: the mind, will, emotion, and body. When I was fully immersed in that lifestyle, my entire identity was wrapped up in my sexual orientation. And the only thing that changed that identity for me was the power of the gospel of Jesus Christ. It required nothing less than a supernatural encounter with the living God. I don't believe true, lasting behavior modification is possible without Holy Spirit transformation.

I'm also not offering a one-size-fits-all approach. There are many different ways to skin this cat. I'm using stories from my own life and from the lives of others to provide and elucidate approaches that I know worked and ones that didn't. I think the experiences God allowed me to go through will help well-meaning pastors and parents avoid common mistakes that end up causing more harm than good.

WHAT NOT TO DO

First, let me start with a story of what I consider to be the wrong way to go about dealing with a son or daughter who comes out.

After much internal debate and contemplation, a friend of mine, Zoë, came out as a lesbian to her Christian parents when she was seventeen years old. This was not an easy decision for her, especially given that she was still in high school and living with her parents. She had been in counseling for a while, and her therapist urged her to be honest with her parents and share what she was going through. So Zoë asked her parents to join her at her therapist's office the next day to discuss a certain matter, but didn't explain beyond that. They were immediately concerned and pleaded with her to tell them what it was about, but she refused, asking them to be patient until the next day.

The following day, Zoë, her parents, and her therapist all met in his office. After settling in, she blurted out, "I'm gay!"

This news came as a shock to her parents, who quickly pushed back, "You're wrong. This is just a phase. This isn't you. How did you even come to this conclusion?"

Zoë told me that her father's expression changed dramatically, and he looked at her as if he'd never known her. Her mother held back tears. They were both flabbergasted by the news. Her father didn't speak to her for the next two weeks. Later they told her they had found a doctor in Arizona who specialized in these kinds of "cases," and convinced her (despite her vehement protestations) to take the trip with them to see this "expert" on reparative therapy. The experience in Arizona was traumatic for Zoë. The first thing the counselor declared to her was that she was not gay, and at one point, he convinced her to let him hold her in his arms like a child. She was enraged by his abrasive, insensitive, and sometimes bizarre therapeutic tactics. After a couple of days of this madness, she demanded to go back home to California.

But after returning home, things got worse. Her parents resorted to punitive measures, and essentially took away all her liberties. They pulled her out of school and attempted to homeschool her to keep a closer tab on her whereabouts. They demanded to know where she was at all times. And on several occasions, her father sat her down with a Bible and angrily detailed the verses that forbid homosexuality, even though she already knew what the Bible and the church had to say on the issue due to her Christian upbringing. He told her she was going to hell if she continued in this lifestyle and threatened several times to kick her out of the house. Once, he told her she had forty-eight hours to move out, and that she would have to become a prostitute or sell drugs on the street to survive.

I understand it's difficult for most parents to learn that their child is gay. I am in no way diminishing the crushing blow this can be to Christian parents. After painstakingly raising up a child in the Lord, to have that child reject all that has been taught at home and in the church can feel like a major betrayal. So there has to be a time of grieving. After all, it is a loss in a way. Parents should allow themselves time to go through this grieving process, and their child needs to understand this as well. But the key here is to *go to the Lord* with the pain. Use the Psalms to aid in crying out to him instead of lashing out at your child. "How long, O LORD? Will you forget me forever? How long will you hide your face from me? How long must I take counsel in my soul and have sorrow in my heart all the day?" (Ps. 13:1–2).

The tendency of the parents is to be reactive and to want to fix the situation immediately. But, as we saw with Zoë, this impulse is harmful and alienating. She'd finally had the courage and vulnerability to share something deeply personal with her parents, and their reaction confirmed her biggest fear about opening up.

A BETTER WAY

Let's take a look at a familiar parable Jesus taught that may be helpful in handling these kinds of situations: the parable of the prodigal son.

> And he said, "There was a man who had two sons. And the younger of them said to his father, 'Father, give me the share of property that is coming to me.' And he divided his property between them. Not many days later, the younger son gathered all he had and took a journey into a far

country, and there he squandered his property in reckless living. And when he had spent everything, a severe famine arose in that country, and he began to be in need. So he went and hired himself out to one of the citizens of that country, who sent him into his fields to feed pigs. And he was longing to be fed with the pods that the pigs ate, and no one gave him anything.

"But when he came to himself, he said, 'How many of my father's hired servants have more than enough bread, but I perish here with hunger! I will arise and go to my father, and I will say to him, "Father, I have sinned against heaven and before you. I am no longer worthy to be called your son. Treat me as one of your hired servants."' And he arose and came to his father. But while he was still a long way off, his father saw him and felt compassion, and ran and embraced him and kissed him. And the son said to him, 'Father, I have sinned against heaven and before you. I am no longer worthy to be called your son.' But the father said to his servants, 'Bring quickly the best robe, and put it on him, and put a ring on his hand, and shoes on his feet. And bring the fattened calf and kill it, and let us eat and celebrate. For this my son was dead, and is alive again; he was lost, and is found.' And they began to celebrate.

"Now his older son was in the field, and as he came and drew near to the house, he heard music and dancing. And he called one of the servants and asked what these things meant. And he said to him, 'Your brother has come, and your father has killed the fattened calf, because he has received him back safe and sound.' But he was angry and refused to go in. His father came out and entreated him, but he answered his father, 'Look, these many years I have served you, and I never disobeyed your command, yet you never gave me a young goat, that I might celebrate with my friends. But when this son of yours came, who has devoured your property with prostitutes, you killed the fattened calf for him!' And he said to him, 'Son, you are always with me, and all that is mine is yours. It was fitting to celebrate and be glad, for this your brother was dead, and is alive; he was lost, and is found.'" (Luke 15:11–32)

In ancient Middle Eastern culture, if a father had two sons, as was the case here, the older would inherit two-thirds of the estate, and the younger, one-third. And it would have been terribly disrespectful for a son to ask for his inheritance *while his father was still alive.* In this honor/shame culture, a scandal like this would have brought disgrace on the entire family. Property in those days was a major part of a man's identity, so taking away part of it would have damaged him not only financially but socially as well. The father's reputation among his friends and community would have been shattered.

The family was also of prime importance in this culture. Your family was an extension of you, and so your children's choices in life directly affected your good standing as an effective and responsible parent. What would everyone think of this father with such a disobedient son? What humiliation!

But notice what happened when the younger son demanded his share of the father's property. What did the father do? His response was more shocking than his son's request! The father simply divided up his property and gave the younger son his portion. That's it. He didn't fly into a violent rage. He didn't punish his son. He didn't ground him. He didn't take away his phone. He didn't admonish him by quoting Bible verses. He didn't try to stop him. He simply let him go.

A GRIEF OBSERVED

Again, I am in no way saying this is easy. When a child comes out to his or her parents, it can be quite a shock. It can feel devastating as it brings up all sorts of emotions: anxiety, fear, anger, disappointment, and so on. This person you have put so much time and energy into raising, and to whom you've imparted your deeply held values and beliefs, is now throwing all that away and going down a path that is antithetical to your faith. How in the world do you handle that? You may be asking, "I've trained up my child in the way she should go, and now she's going to depart from it?" Or, "I've done my part. Why isn't my child doing his?" Remember, the proverb, "Train up a child in the way he should go; even when he is old he will not depart from it" (Prov. 22:6), is a *principle*, not a promise.

I mentioned earlier that parents would do well to take the time to go through the grieving process. This is what it was like for the father in Jesus' parable. When his younger son returned home, he told his older son, "This your brother was *dead*, and is alive; he was lost, and is found" (Luke 15:32, emphasis mine). According to Jesus, having a child refuse to follow the path you've set as a parent is analogous to having a death in the family. This can be difficult, but the way you respond is important.

It's not uncommon for Christians to behave like the older brother in this parable. They are irritated that someone so undeserving, so loathsome (like a homosexual man who was engaged in that life for years but then repents) is suddenly given grace by God and accepted into his arms. They have a sense of entitlement (just like the older brother) and have convinced themselves that they are somehow better— that they have merited their own salvation, even though it is *only* by God's grace that they themselves are saved. "By grace you have been saved through faith. And this is not your own doing; it is the gift of God, not a result of works, so that no one may boast" (Eph. 2:8–9). We need to be reminded of this truth daily.

Sometimes, while driving through West Hollywood or wherever and I see two gay men holding hands, I find myself rolling my eyes and thinking, *C'mon, guys! Don't you know that homosexual behavior is wrong? Don't you see how destructive it is?* Then I catch myself and have to repent. Even I, the younger brother, can easily become the older brother in a split second.

It is good for children who come out to their parents to be patient as well. They need to give their parents the time to process and grieve. In my experience, children who come out to their parents expect them to be fully on board *immediately*. They don't understand why their parents wouldn't join PFLAG (Parents, Families, and Friends of Lesbians and Gays) right away or attend a gay pride event the following June. The reason for this disconnect is because while they grew up dealing with same-sex attractions their whole life, and by the time they muster the courage to tell their parents, they have already gone through years of wrestling with the issue on their own or with close friends, their parents had no idea. They expect their parents to be up to speed on what they have been struggling with all their life right away.

Remember, though you may have come to terms with your sexual orientation, your parents were (usually) completely in the dark about it. And you coming out may be the first time they have ever even considered that their child might be gay. It's unfair for you to expect your parents to be cool with it seconds after you've told them.

Both sides need to be patient with each other. This is a complicated issue, and rash judgments won't help anyone. Cooler heads will ultimately prevail.

EAT, PRAY, LOVE

My sister-in-law, Kim, is a great example of how a Christian family member should respond to this issue. She has been a strong believer since early in her childhood. I met her when I was in high school, and she started dating my older brother, Greg. She and I always had a special bond; we enjoyed chatting and hanging out with each other.

Years later, after I came out as gay to my whole family, my relationship with Kim remained the same, even though she was what I would have called a Bible-thumping, evangelical Christian. I never felt an ounce of condemnation from her. She never sat me down to explain to me that I was sinning. She never quoted Bible verses to me. She never judged me for my lifestyle. Instead, she did something far more dangerous: she prayed . . . for twenty years! (Please note that I'm not suggesting that there are not times when difficult truths must be spoken clearly and honestly. There is certainly a time and a place for that, but the key is doing so in love.)

Over the years, while in Los Angeles, I would go back to Dallas for Christmas (if not New York). One of the highlights of my visits was getting together with Kim at the nearest Starbucks. We would chat for hours. I would talk about guys; she would talk about God. She was genuinely interested in my life, and never once said to me, "You know, you're still sinning." I knew that she knew that I knew that she believed homosexuality was a sin. She never told me this explicitly, but because she was an evangelical Christian, it was obvious to me where she stood on this issue.

She was very open about her faith and would talk about what God was doing in her life. But this didn't bother me, because I sensed an unconditional love from her. Her love for me didn't increase or decrease based on whether or not I was in a relationship with a guy at that particular moment. In other words, she didn't withhold love from me because of the way I lived my life. She did two key things throughout the years: she loved me unconditionally and prayed for me without ceasing! That's it. When I let Kim and my brother know about my conversion to Christianity, they were beyond thrilled. Joyous tears abounded.

The way Kim treated me through the years created a deep trust between us. I knew I could tell her anything and not feel judged. I appreciated that she was unapologetic about her convictions as a Christian yet didn't try to bludgeon me with those convictions. You might be saying, "Yeah, but she was your sister-in-law, not your mother or father." I don't disagree that it's much harder on a parent. But as hard as it may be, imitating Kim's approach as a parent ultimately will be much more helpful than harmful, for everyone involved.

A PASTOR'S CARE

The pastor of Reality LA, Tim Chaddick, who preached that inspiring sermon on that pivotal day that forever changed my life, was extremely helpful to me as a new believer coming out of that lifestyle. (He moved to London to plant Reality Church London in 2016.) When I met him in 2009, soon after I got saved, we exchanged phone numbers and began meeting for coffee on a regular basis. What struck me most about Tim was his empathy. I felt deeply supported and loved, despite my wild and depraved past. Tim, having grown up near San Francisco, was no stranger to gay culture; this terrain was in no way foreign to him.

I think that's why he was such a great pastor and friend. He had a soft spot for men and women whom God had saved out of that life. Actually, he had a soft spot for the LGBT community in general. He knew how to communicate with me and others in that community and with those freshly rescued out of it. Over the years, I witnessed Tim interacting with many still in or coming out of the LGBT community with such grace and compassion that he demonstrated for me what it meant to "love your neighbor as yourself" (Matt. 19:19). Yes, he was clear about his convictions. But he spoke "the truth *in love*" (Eph. 4:15). And that made all the difference.

Tim was also very open about his own debauched past before coming to Christ. In fact, his vulnerability and transparency from the pulpit created an environment where congregants felt comfortable confessing their sins to one another and being honest about the daily struggles of following Christ. "We're all broken, and we need Jesus" was the perennial motto at Reality LA. We all knew that when we came in through those doors on Sunday, we could be utterly honest about our failings that week. This culture of transparency, confession, and forgiveness gave all of us the license to be real. I never felt singled out because of my past. I learned that everyone has a past, but that Jesus is sanctifying our present.

This is what I appreciated most about Tim as a pastor: he wasn't interested in just playing church. He wanted real transformation to occur in us by being real, not only with God, but also with each other. How can we bear one another's burdens if we don't know what they are?

SAME BUT DIFFERENT

I often hear from Christians that homosexual behavior is no different from any other sin. Yes, it is the same in that all sin is an offense to God, from stealing to murder to greed. But no, there is a difference (and it's no small difference) in that homosexuality has become an identity, not just a sin.

Again, there are gay pride parades but not gossip pride parades. Homosexuality is so deeply tied to one's essence that it's very difficult to untangle this particular sin from the person who is engaging in it. It takes a lot of love and patience, not to mention the power of the Holy Spirit, to help someone break free from this sin/identity. We, as the church, must strive to treat those who struggle with this sin with more care, and those in the LGBT community with Christlike love.

I was recently invited to a small dinner party at an incredibly beautiful home in Malibu. A friend from church worked for the owner, who was a gay man. Much to my friend's and my surprise (and joy!), the owner wanted to hear more about Christianity. He was curious as to why two gay guys would give up that life to follow Christ. Of course, we were more than happy to have this opportunity to share the gospel with this group of relatively hardened skeptics, both gay and straight. The only problem was that our gracious host had failed to mention to his friends that two evangelical Christians, who had both been *saved out of the homosexual life*, were the guests of honor!

When, immediately after the first course was served, our host turned to me and asked if I would share my story with everyone, I almost choked on my fennel salad. But as I was detailing the story of my conversion, I saw a look of genuine interest on the faces of the listeners; that is, until one of them asked the question I always get: "What about your sexuality?"

As I addressed that issue, there was a sudden shift in the room. The mood quickly changed from polite interest to semi-hostile disgust. I tried my best to explain why homosexual behavior was incompatible with Christianity, when suddenly the discussion at the table became very animated. Various guests were chiming in with their own views, not only on this incendiary subject but on "spirituality" in general. After our second course, the conversation started to become heated. So much so that at one point, when I felt like it was getting out of hand, I stopped everyone and said: "Guys, guys. I just want you all to know that the *only* reason I drove an hour out to Malibu on a school night during midterms is because *I love you!* That's it. I'm not here to win an argument. I'm here because I love you. Period."

Everyone was taken aback by this unexpected expression of my motives. A few of them seemed dumbstruck. The temperature in the room instantly dropped, bonhomie was quickly restored, and the evening ended on a good note.

We didn't experience a mass conversion that evening, but I was thankful for the opportunity to share what God has done in my life.

Dear reader,

I would say the same to you. My motivation for writing this book is not to win a debate. It is not so I could be right and you wrong. More than anything, my hope is that you will come away with a better understanding of this complex issue, from every angle, so you can make informed choices that affect eternity. I hope I was able to help you, in some way, to grasp the truth regarding homosexuality, or to maybe become aware of some blind spots you hadn't considered before.

After sharing my faith on several occasions with an

ex-boyfriend in New York, I later texted him the following: "On the last day, you will understand how much I loved you."

He responded, "Thank you, Becket."

And that is truly my motivation for writing this book: *love*.

Yours in Christ,

Becket

ACKNOWLEDGMENTS

I would like to express my sincerest gratitude and deepest appreciation to the following friends:

Jenny Baumgartner, for being a rock star editor and believing in this book.

The whole outstanding team at Thomas Nelson, including Sujin Hong, Aryn Van Dyke, Sara Broun, and Rachel Tockstein.

Don Gates, for being the best agent a writer could ask for (such a boss!).

Francis Chan, for your amazing support for this book and for your great generosity over the years.

Mark Beuving, for your generous heart and wonderful edits.

Zach Moore, for your rigorous and insightful notes. Your friendship is a blessing.

Aly Wicker and Janelle Henson, for your valuable input.

All my brilliant professors at Talbot School of Theology, including Rob Price, Mark Saucy, and J. P. Moreland.

ACKNOWLEDGMENTS

Tim Chaddick, for preaching the sermon that led to my salvation and for your wonderful friendship. "How beautiful are the feet of those who preach the good news!" (Rom. 10:15).

Nick Tortorice, for your great friendship and all your prayer and wisdom over the years.

Jeremy Treat, for your steadfast and excellent leadership at Reality LA (and for connecting me to Don Gates).

Sean and Cate Johnson, for your love and support throughout seminary.

Maggy Wong, for your unfailing encouragement.

Chelsey Holmlund, for your friendship and countless prayer sessions.

The awesome and relentless intercessors: Sara Rae Darabont, Joni Sobels, and Genevieve Giordano.

Annie Ing, for being a great prayer warrior and friend during this whole process.

Stephen Baldwin, for your huge support and friendship.

Caleb Kaltenbach, for championing this book.

All who generously supported me financially for and during my seminary: Greg and Kim Cook, Francis and Lisa Chan, Kim and Anne Storm, William and Susan Brick, Shirley Luthi-Cox, Tim and Wendy Kane, Harry and Cici Scott, Carter and Season De Angelis, David and Cindy Scholl, and Reality LA.

Rob Bylett, for your brilliant cover design.

NOTES

CHAPTER 1: BEING THERE

1. Karl Marx, "A Contribution to the Critique of Hegel's Philosophy of Right," *Deutsch-Französische Jahrbücher*, 7 & 10 February 1844, Paris.
2. Richard Dawkins, in a debate with the Archbishop of York, Dr. John Habgood, on the existence of God. Edinburgh Science Festival, 1992.

CHAPTER 2: *DEUS EX MACHINA: CONVERSION*

1. John Wesley, *Journal of John Wesley* (Oxford: Oxford University Press, 1987).
2. C. S. Lewis, *Mere Christianity* (New York: Touchstone, 1996), 85.
3. John Calvin, *Institutes of the Christian Religion*, ed. John T. McNeill, trans. Ford Lewis Battles (Louisville, KY: Westminster John Knox Press, 1960), 1:76.

CHAPTER 4: COLLEGE YEARS: GOD IS DEAD

1. Evelyn Waugh, *Brideshead Revisited* (Boston: Little, Brown and Company, 1973), 85–86.

CHAPTER 6: SLOUCHING TOWARD HOLLYWOOD

1. Victor Frankl, *Man's Search for Meaning* (Boston: Beacon Press, 2006), 37.
2. Evelyn Waugh, *Brideshead Revisited* (Boston: Little, Brown and Company, 1973), 45.
3. Ben Brantley, "Sam Shepard, Actor and Pulitzer-Winning Playwright, Is Dead at 73," *New York Times*, July 31, 2017, www.nytimes.com/2017/07/31/theater/sam-shepard-dead.html?hpw&rref=obituaries&action=click&pgtype=Homepage&module=well-region&region=bottom-well&WT.nav=bottom-well.

CHAPTER 7: IS THAT ALL THERE IS?

1. C. S. Lewis, *The Weight of Glory* (New York: HarperOne, 2001), 42–43.
2. Leo Tolstoy, *A Confession*, trans. Aylmer Maude (Mineola, NY: Dover Publications, 2005), 17.

CHAPTER 9: JUST THE FAQS

1. Robert R. Reilly, *Making Gay Okay: How Rationalizing Homosexual Behavior Is Changing Everything* (San Francisco: Ignatius Press, 2015), 131.
2. Wikipedia, s.v. "Biology and Sexual Orientation," accessed November 16, 2018, https://en.wikipedia.org/wiki/Biology_and_sexual_orientation.
3. Emily Dickinson, "Letters from Dickinson to Mary Bowles," spring 1862, accessed November 16, 2018, http://archive.emilydickinson.org/correspondence/mbowles/l262.html.

CHAPTER 10: YOUNG AND RICH

1. Bari M. Schwartz, "Hot or Not? Website Briefly Judges Looks," *Harvard Crimson*, November 4, 2003, www.thecrimson.com/article/2003/11/4/hot-or-not-website-briefly-judges/?page=single.

2. Alyson Shontell, "This Man Lost Out on $3 Billion by Following His Father's Advice," *Business Insider*, May 16, 2012, www.businessinsider.com/joe-green-missed-facebook -opportunity-2012-5.

3. Robert H. Stein, *New American Commentary: Luke* (Nashville: Broadman Press, 1992), 24:457.

CHAPTER 11: BAD SOUP

1. Philip Ziegler, *King Edward VIII* (New York: Alfred A. Knopf, 1990), 193–290.

2. Tremper Longman III, *Genesis: The Story of God Bible Commentary* (Grand Rapids: Zondervan, 2016), 332.

3. Gordon J. Wenham, *Genesis 16–50: Word Biblical Commentary* (Nashville: Nelson, 1994), 2:175.

4. Longman, *Genesis*, 332.

5. Bruce K. Waltke, *Genesis: A Commentary* (Grand Rapids: Zondervan, 2001), 361.

6. Kenneth A. Mathews, *Genesis 11:27–50:26, The New American Commentary*, vol. 1b (Nashville: B&H, 2005), 394.

7. Victor P. Hamilton, *The Book of Genesis: Chapters 18–50, The New International Commentary on the Old Testament* (Grand Rapids: Eerdmans, 1995), 185.

8. Waltke, *Genesis*, 363.

9. Mark Saucy, "The Promises of the Abrahamic Covenant," Lecture at Talbot School of Theology, La Mirada, California, April 14, 2015.

10. "A Despised Birthright," Ligonier Ministries, accessed December 10, 2018, www.ligonier.org/learn/devotionals /despised-birthright.

11. Esau ended up marrying two Hittite women, much to the chagrin of his parents: "They made life bitter for Isaac and Rebekah" (Gen. 26:35). Rebekah told Isaac, "I loathe my life because of the Hittite women" (Gen. 27:46).

Esau must have known that his grandfather, Abraham, did everything in his power to prevent his son, Isaac, from marrying a Canaanite woman; that the Hittites were listed among the wicked Canaanites; and that marrying these women was forbidden: "You shall not intermarry with them, giving your daughters to their sons or taking their daughters for your sons" (Deut. 7:3). He also must have known that God condemned these people for their wickedness and would eventually give Abraham's offspring their land (Gen. 15:17–20).

So by marrying these women, Esau was essentially thumbing his nose at Abraham's vision—and, of course, God's promise—concerning Israel's destiny (Waltke, *Genesis*, 375–76). Isaac and Rebekah, like King George V and Queen Mary, grieved deeply over their sons' dishonorable decisions.

12. Matthew Henry, *Commentary on Genesis 25:29–34*, Blue Letter Bible, accessed December 10, 2018, www.blueletterbible.org/Comm/mhc/Gen/Gen_025.cfm.

13. Waltke, *Genesis*, 377.

14. John Bunyan, *The Pilgrim's Progress*, ed. Roger Pooley (London: Penguin Classics, 2008), 37.

15. Bunyan, *Pilgrim's Progress*, 37.

16. Bunyan, *Pilgrim's Progress*, 37–38.

17. Bunyan, *Pilgrim's Progress*, 38.

18. Tim Keller, *Reason for God* (New York: Penguin Random House, 2008), 179–80.

19. Matthew Henry, *Commentary on Numbers 20:14–21*, Blue Letter Bible, accessed December 10, 2018, www.blueletterbible.org/Comm/mhc/Num/Num_020.cfm.

20. John Calvin, *Commentaries on the First Book of Moses Called Genesis* (Grand Rapids: Eerdmans, 1948), 2:53.

CHAPTER 12: THREE GUYS AND A FURNACE

1. Andrew E. Hill, *The Expositor's Bible Commentary: Daniel–Malachi*, ed. Tremper Longman III and David E. Garland, 8th ed. (Grand Rapids: Zondervan, 2008), 45.

2. Iain M. Duguid, *Daniel: Reformed Expository Commentary* (Phillipsburg, NJ: P&R, 2008), 9.

3. Hill, *Expositor's Bible Commentary*, 49.

4. Duguid, *Daniel*, 9.

5. Eugene Carpenter, *Cornerstone Biblical Commentary*, ed. Philip W. Comfort (Carol Stream, IL: Tyndale, 2010), 9:319.

6. John Calvin, *Commentaries on the Book of the Prophet Daniel*, *Calvin's Commentaries*, trans. Thomas Myers (Grand Rapids: Eerdmans, 1948), 1:97–8. See also Hill, *Expositor's Bible Commentary*, 53.

7. Hill, *Expositor's Bible Commentary*, 76.

8. Hill, *Expositor's Bible Commentary*, 76.

9. Duguid, *Daniel*, 47.

10. Hill, *Expositor's Bible Commentary*, 77.

11. Calvin, *Commentaries on the Book of the Prophet Daniel*, 1:215.

12. Matthew Henry, *Matthew Henry's Commentary on the Whole Bible, Isaiah to Malachi* (Old Tappan, NJ: Fleming H. Revell Company, 1708–1710), 4:1016.

13. Calvin, *Commentaries on the Book of the Prophet Daniel*, 1:219.

14. Duguid, *Daniel*, 56.

15. Martin Brecht, *Oxford Encyclopedia of the Reformation*, ed. Hans J. Hillerbrand, trans. Wolfgang Katenz (New York: Oxford University Press, 1996), s.v. "Luther, Martin," 1:460.

16. Matthew Vines makes these arguments in *God and the Gay Christian* (New York: Convergent, 2014), 11.

17. Mary Eberstadt, "Regular Christians Are No Longer Welcome in American Culture," *Time*, June 29, 2016, http://time.com /4385755/faith-in-america/?xid=time_socialflow_twitter.

18. David F. Wells, *God in the Wasteland* (Grand Rapids: Eerdmans, 1994), 29.
19. Duguid, *Daniel*, 58.

ABOUT THE AUTHOR

Becket Cook was born and raised in Dallas, Texas. He moved to Los Angeles after college to pursue a career in writing and acting. He currently works as a production designer in the fashion world. In 2017, Cook received an MA in Theology from Talbot School of Theology at Biola University, and spends much of his time in ministry, speaking on the issue of homosexuality at churches, universities, and conferences.